go to BED *with*

# JONATHAN
# ROSS

A Virgin Book
Published in 1988
by the Paperback Division of
W.H. Allen & Co Plc
44 Hill Street
London W1X 8LB

Typeset by Creative Text
Printed in Great Britain by Scotprint Ltd,
Musselburgh

ISBN 0 86369 283 4

The Archive Photos were kindly provided by Syndication International; London Features International and Rex Features.

## PUBLISHER'S NOTE

What book would be complete without a foreword! Not this one, because today's the print deadline and we're still one page short.

We'd therefore like to take this opportunity to invite you, the reader, to slip between the covers of this book and discover for yourself some of Jonathan Ross's special little secrets.

In these excerpts from diaries spanning the last twenty-three years Jonathan exposes many of his hitherto totally private parts — his thoughts, hopes, fears and experiences.

This is the true story of a Leytonstone lad's long, hard and sometimes painful journey through life. So have your hanky ready because JR is about to spill the beans.

## JONATHAN ROSS

Hello and welcome to my bed,

All of human life is here — romance, heartache, the years of suffering and poverty, the fleeting moments of fame and, of course, the death of my goldfish.

Remember, a problem shared is a problem halved and if enough people buy this bed I'll hardly have any problems left at all or, as my mum used to say

Goodnight, God bless, sweet repose
Half the bed and all the clothes,

*Jonathan*

JONATHAN

# THE LAS' WEEZORT

Hello evweebod' peeps, an' whelk to the Jonathan Woss book wiv me as you fame sexy-hip host. I'm hope you got a needaw an' fwed handy cos you gonna split you sides lawfin'.

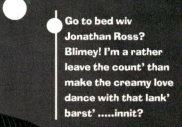

Go to bed wiv Jonathan Ross? Blimey! I'm a rather leave the count' than make the creamy love dance with that lank' barst' .....innit?

# CONTENTS

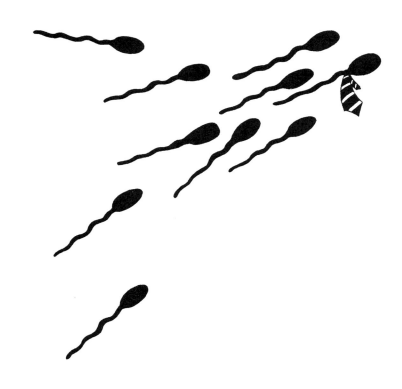

# CHAPTER ONE

## 1960-1968

### Life Before Long Trousers

# CERTIFIED COPY of an ENTRY OF BIRTH
## Pursuant to the Births and Deaths Registration Act, 1953

### Registration District CAMDEN

| No. | When and where born | Name, if any | Sex | Name of father | Name of mother | Height | Weight | Lapels |
|-----|---------------------|--------------|-----|----------------|----------------|--------|--------|--------|
| Columns:– 1 | | 2 | 3 | 4 | 5 | 6 | 7 | 8 |
| 100 | Seventeenth November 1960 Camden, London, NW 1 | Jonathan ROSS | Boy | Mr ROSS | Mrs ROSS | 15" | 8lbs 2oz | Wide |

*Registrar of Births and Deaths*

WITNESS MY HAND this **1st** day of **December** 19 60

The statutory fee for this certificate is 3s. 9d.
Where a search is necessary to find the entry,
a search fee is payable in addition.

**NOVEMBER 22nd**

**1963**

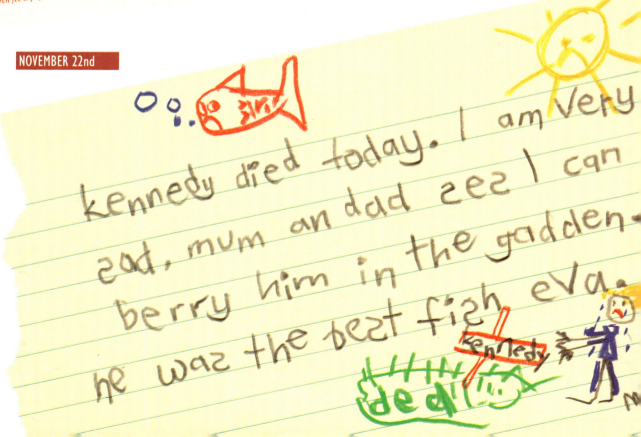

kennedy died today. I am very sad, mum an dad sez I can berry him in the gadden. he waz the best fish eva.

dear santer

pleez may I have
some long trowzez but
not just any oled
rubbizh I heer there
iz a zail at
eevzan le ron

1965

first Dave Scool
Deer diry, today I god to scool
first time my teecher is name
Mis Frost she has glasses and
a big stick my bes friend is
called Brain Dickins he gave me
some peecess of cak but all uthus
are hobble I don lik them they
dont no the meening of stile

me

10

## 1966

**JULY 30th**　England won the World Cup today and I got so excited that I rushed upstairs to play with my World Cup Willie. Mum says not to do this as it will make me go blind – I think she's confused with wanking.

## 1967

'Tweading the boards'

**MAY 10th**　Met a kindly old gentleman on the way home from school today. He said I could be in his football team, as I was just the sort of little boy he liked – I didn't even have to have a trial! All he wanted was for me to sit in his lap whilst he made sure I wasn't ticklish in certain places, as he said that football players often suffer from this and it can affect their game. I told the old pervert to piss off.

**MAY 11th**　Told mum about the football man today. She wouldn't stop asking me questions about him, and then she told me that a funny man in a blue Noddy car was coming round to ask me some more questions about my special footballing friend. I think she meant the Old Bill were coming round to quiz me about "Mr Pervy". When is she going to grow up?

**JUNE 10th**　Auditioned for a part in our school production of *Othello* today. I did the Wodwego on the Wialto speech. It went really great and I got in lots of arm movements. We will find out who plays what on Friday. I'm a cert for Othello.

**JUNE 12th**　Have been offered the part of "Boy who shows audience to their seats." Mrs Shorter says this is a very important role, vital to the play, and the best news of all, he gets to wear a suit instead of stupid ladies' tights. Have flicked through the play – in terms of lines it's a smallish part, but nevertheless a great challenge.

**JUNE 13th**　I am not at all depressed. I never wanted to play silly old Othello anyway.

**DECEMBER 11th** Hooray, it's Wednesday, and nearly time for my favourite programme *Call My Bluff* with the fantabulous Frank "Everyone's a fruit and nut case" Muir.

16.12.67

**BBC**

Dear Mrs Ross,

Thank you for your letter dated 9 May 1966, I apologise for the delay but things have been a bit hectic of late.

I would like to make it clear that the corporation cannot be held responsible for any effects, adverse or otherwise, caused by Mr Frank Muir's appearance on television, which allegedly scared your son.

If you feel that his impediment is serious, may I then suggest the help of a speech therapist, failing that I would be most happy to come round and have a chat with the young chap myself.

Yours sincerely,

David Bellamy (Public Relations)

**JUNE 6th**      Kennedy died today. He was my favourite hamster, I named him after a goldfish I used to have.

**AUGUST 25th**      Went to Czechoslovakia for my summer holidays. Mum was sick on the plane and I met some nice Russians in Prague, otherwise all very uneventful.

**'On the whole an uneventful year'**

**OCTOBER 12th**      The fab Leapy Lee is at number two in the pop chart with my fave song, 'Little Arrows'. I couldn't wait to get home and tell Sue about it, she's still an Elvis fan and whenever I mention Leapy Lee she just stands in front of the telly so I can't watch *Father, Dear Father.*

Sis wasn't pleased at all, she pulled my hair and told me Leapy Lee was a one-hit wonder before storming upstairs to listen to her tranny.

**OCTOBER 13th**      Saw my chance for revenge. Mum and dad were watching the boring Olympics on TV, so Sue and me went upstairs to listen to Fab 208 Radio Luxembourg. While Sue was getting all soppy and sissy over the latest Dave, Dee, Dozy, Beaky, Mick and Tich record I got to work on her copy of 'Love Me Tender' with my chemistry set. I burnt a great big hole in the bit where fat old Elvis sings 'love me sweet'.

Sent to bed early. I heard dad tell mum she was spoiling me, and that 1/6d was too much pocket money for a boy of my age.

**OCTOBER 14th**      Dad took me to the barber's and asked for a 'College Boy'. But all that happened is that my hair got chopped off. I didn't like my new so-called haircut, but I have to keep in dad's good books, it's my birthday next month.

(continued) Sue and me played a new game tonight; Leapy Lee versus Elvis Presley. It's easy, you get a piece of paper and fold it in half. On one side of the paper I wrote all the things I liked about the unbeatable Leapy Lee, on the other side of the paper Sue wrote down all the things she liked about silly old Elvis.

Leapy is not a soppy Yank.

Both of Leapy's names begin with L, Elvis's don't.

Leapy comes from Eastbourne. I went there once with my mum and dad, lots of old people took all the deck chairs.

Leapy's the first pop star to run a Bingo Hall, even Dickie Valentine hasn't done that.

Leapy left school at 15 and didn't have to do Latin O-level.

Elvis was very manly in the film 'Tickle Me'.

Elvis can wiggle his pelvis.

Elvis lives in a big mansion in America with a beautiful wife.

Elvis is the biggest selling pop star in the whole world.

I think Elvis has a degree in Advanced Physics, at least that's what Mary Greaves told me.

Sue and me are not talking to each other. I have given my copy of 'Little Arrows' to the Salvation Army and have joined the Herman's Hermits Fan Club. Dad has thrown my chemistry set away.

# CHAPTER TWO

## 1969-1979

### The Spotty Years

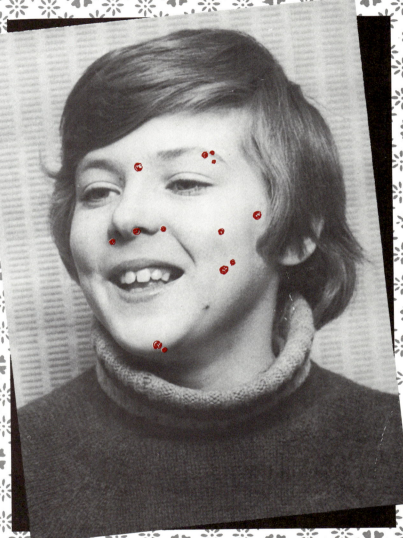

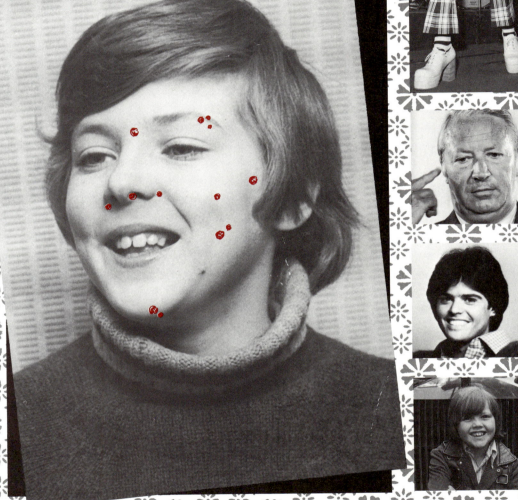

**MAY 11th** V. boring day at school. During afternoon break Brendan McVitie and me made Barry Kepple's sister Susie eat a live worm. She cried and cried – it was great. Later played with Barry's silly putty and I showed him and Brendan some of my more avant-garde designs for the juniors' soccer kit. I feel that the addition of lime green and purple would jazz up what is, let's face it, one of the more conservative strips in third-form football.

**MAY 12th** Felt a strange, but not unpleasant, throbbing sensation in my pants during Maths this afternoon. This Italian cotton certainly seems to be living up to its promises. Hope the replacement teacher, Miss Bagshaw, didn't notice – she seemed to look at me rather oddly when she leant over to correct my calculus. Maybe I bought them in the wrong size?

**MAY 13th** Funny, I dreamt about that new Maths teacher Miss Bagshaw last night. Must remember to complain to mum about her shoddy washing methods, which seem to be leaving horrid stains all over my new Paisley pyjamas.

**MAY 14th** Seem to be enjoying school more than usual at the moment for some reason. Even Maths wasn't as bad as usual – that Miss Bagshaw certainly knows how to explain trigonometry to a chap – but I think I must have eaten something bad at lunch because when she was talking to me I went all sweaty and she sent me to the sick room.

**MAY 15th** Saturday – what a drag. Can't wait to get back to school and practise my quadratic equations. Spent the day round at the McVities' house with Brendan. He got a Spirograph for his birthday so we played with it for at least twenty minutes before it broke. At tea-time a couple of friends of Brendan's father came round and asked him to go for a nice drive in the country with them, but funnily enough he didn't seem at all keen. Far from it. He just kept whimpering and saying, "Reggie, please … I never laid a finger on the black cash box … I swear to you, Ron … on my mother's life, Ron ..." Honestly – grown-ups can be so forgetful! Lucky I was there to point out to Mr McVitie that Brendan and I had helped him bury a small black

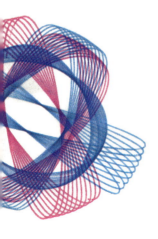

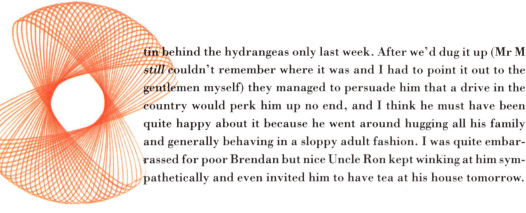

tin behind the hydrangeas only last week. After we'd dug it up (**Mr M** *still* couldn't remember where it was and I had to point it out to the gentlemen myself) they managed to persuade him that a drive in the country would perk him up no end, and I think he must have been quite happy about it because he went around hugging all his family and generally behaving in a sloppy adult fashion. I was quite embarrassed for poor Brendan but nice Uncle Ron kept winking at him sympathetically and even invited him to have tea at his house tomorrow.

**MAY 16th** Brendan asked me if I wanted to accompany him to his Uncle Ron's house for tea but mum said I had to do my Geography homework instead after what Miss Philipson wrote in my report last term about me being so bad at the subject I get lost on the way to the lessons ha ha. Who does she think she is, Tony Blackburn? After supper I rang Brendan's house to see how it went and his mother answered in this peculiar voice and said, "Brendan who? No one by that name lives here thank you and I never saw anything, promise." Maybe it's her Thyme of the Month.

**MAY 17th** How can I ever have thought Maths was a boring subject? Either I was mad or it took someone of Miss Bagshaw's calibre to make me see how fascinating and Now it really is. I think tomorrow I'll ask her if I can have some extra lessons after school and maybe do my Maths O-level a year early. Who knows – I might even be a child prodigy. Brendan was off sick today but I went round Barry's place to watch *The Tomorrow People* after school. What a fantastic programme and very educational as well, as I'm sure enlightened and With It teachers like Miss Bagshaw would agree.

**MAY 18th** If I live to be 35 I'll never forget the look on Miss Bagshaw's face as she threw me out of the classroom this afternoon. I tried to explain about Chris Whatley putting itching powder down the front of my pants but somehow I don't think she was listening. Later I got sent to see the Games master Mr Reid who gave me a weird talk all about the connection between PE and Man's immortal soul. After school I tried ringing Brendan to tell him about it but some funny man with a deep voice answered the phone and said the whole McVitie family had moved home to some lake or other. I think I might enrol in circuit training.

# CANTERTOYS UK LTD

Dear Mr Ross,

Thank you for your latest letter regarding the Action Man toy manufactured by Cantertoys UK Ltd. While we fully appreciate your comments about the cut and quality of the available costumes, we would like to point out that to our knowledge few French resistance fighters patronised Saville Row tailors, moreover a Thai silk lining with a credit-card pocket is not a usual feature of a flak jacket.

We have returned your designs as to date we have no plans for an Action Man Haute Couture Spring collection.

Yours faithfully,

*Barry Gaultier*

Barry Gaultier, Consumer relations

PS Thank you for your photograph of 'Dan in eau de nil evening wrap'.

**AUGUST 31st**    Took my Action Man, Dan, to Greenspan's bespoke Gentlemen's Outfitters today after receiving a disappointing letter from Cantertoys (enclosed) informing me they wouldn't be using my designs. Mr Greenspan agreed that the storm-trooper uniform was a disgrace, and although I couldn't agree with his view that Dan hasn't got the height to carry off double-breasted, I was impressed by his suggestion of the new lighter Italian silks which I think will be particularly flattering to Dan's colouring. In the end we agreed on one double-breasted, one silk single-breasted, a blazer, and two pairs of slacks. Only a fortnight till it's all ready, put it on mum's bill.

**SEPTEMBER 15th**    Got the new gear from Greenspan's today; it all fits beautifully. Showed him off to everyone at school – Chris Whatley says he looks like a ponce, and wouldn't let Dan join in with the others – I don't want him playing with that rough lot anyhow. Mr Lucas the nice English teacher was the complete opposite. He kept asking me loads of questions about Dan's gear, like why I was so concerned that he wore natural fibres next to his skin and when exactly did Dan tell me he was allergic to polyester? It was a nice change to talk to someone intelligent other than Dan.

**SEPTEMBER 22nd** Got a letter from the school today – Dan has been given an appointment with the school psychiatrist – I suppose I'll have to go with him. I thought mum was upset about the letter from school until she opened the one from Mr Greenspan, then I realised what "upset" really means. Just because she can't be bothered to make nice clothes for my Action Man I don't see why she has to go mad about me getting someone else to do it.

**OCTOBER 3rd** Saw the psychiatrist today. Nice bloke, although like all shrinks a bit on the mad side. Mum has to go and see him next and not before time.

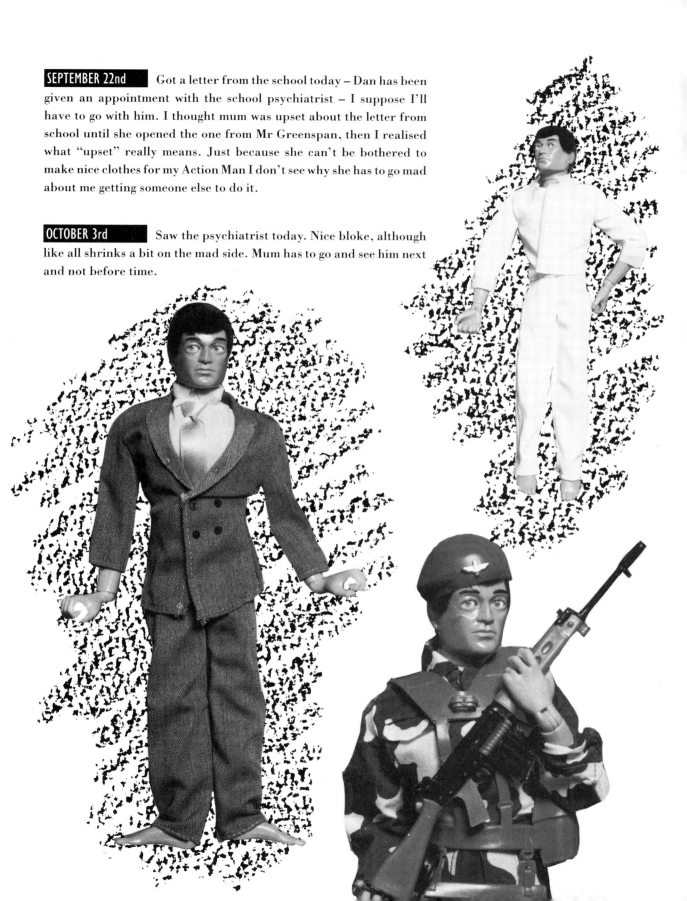

**JANUARY 4th** Had gym today. Climbed the rope which is something I haven't done for years. It was strangely satisfying.

**JANUARY 16th** Climbed the rope fifteen times today. I really enjoyed it although I am finding myself getting rather breathless at the top which is rather strange because I'm definitely using the correct technique of gripping the rope firmly between my legs and then hauling myself up.

**JANUARY 17th** Was banned from using the rope today after the teacher said my moaning when I got to the top was distracting the girls' netball team.

**JANUARY 20th** Was caught trying to use the rope at lunchtime today by Mr Reid. He took me into his office and started to give me one of his lectures – something about …the body being a temple… I think he's bonkers – I was only wanking myself off.

**FEBRUARY 26th** Meet me on the corner when the lights are going down and I'll be there, yes I promise I'll be there. How can anyone feel downhearted when there are groups like Lindisfarne in the world?

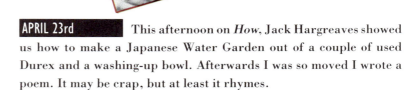

**APRIL 23rd** This afternoon on *How*, Jack Hargreaves showed us how to make a Japanese Water Garden out of a couple of used Durex and a washing-up bowl. Afterwards I was so moved I wrote a poem. It may be crap, but at least it rhymes.

# 'Fun with Dick and Gym'

**1972**

# owed to Spring

by Jonathan Ross

Ah me!
Sometimes I wish I could be
Just like a tree –
Instead of my arms, its branches
Instead of my legs, its trunk
Instead of my trunk, a bit
more of its trunk.
On my head there are
hundreds of green leaves,
And a bird is perching on
my face.
O, What a wonderful thing
is nature.

**SEPTEMBER 11th** Am I the only fourteen year old who cares about planet Earth and what's going on here? Spent summer holidays reading the works of Herman Hesse, Søren Aabye Kierkegaard and Alasdair Maclean. Now I'm looking forward to school and discussing some of the more revolutionary world philosophies with my contemporaries.

**SEPTEMBER 15th** Since term started there's only been one topic of conversation. Malcolm Hargreaves said he Did It in a caravan site in Clacton, Jeremy Trott claims to have Done It in his own kitchen, and I gather Spunky Mayhew Does It with great relish. What on earth is "It"? I need some advice v. quickly. I don't want my chums to think I'm ignorant.

**SEPTEMBER 16th** Today Malcolm asked me if I'd Done It, so naturally I said I had. He said how often? I said all the time, but only when I'm alone. Now no one will talk to me and they all snigger every time I walk by and shout out things about one of the presenters of *Magpie*. It's all so confusing – what's Susan Stranks got to do with all this?

# Celebrity Cockney Rhyming Slang

**Eartha Kitt:** as in "Open a window, will you – I'm just off for an Eartha." A common variation is **Ingrid (Pitt)**; when used as an adjective either **Conway (Twitty)** or **Walter (Mitty)** as in **"Terry and June** is one of the Walteriest programmes ever."

**Susan Stranks:** First used on Thames TV circa 1969: "And before every episode of *Magpie*, Mick Robertson Susan Stranks."

**Paul Anka:** As in "Jeremy Beadle is a complete Paul Anka."

**Gareth Hunt:** As in "Gareth Hunt is a complete Gareth Hunt."

**Jeremy Beadle:** As in "Jeremy Beadle – what a C**t."

**NOVEMBER 13th** Went to a speech therapist after my mother decided there was something wrong with the way I talked. The lesson ended rather abruptly after I told the therapist my problem seemed to be that I couldn't get my tongue round my "R's". He went all red and started shouting something about "youth of today... no respect... too much television" and the next thing I knew I was out on the pavement. Cheered myself up on the way home by popping into the local record store and buying Marie Osmond's latest single 'Paper Woses' – I don't know why but this sort of thing really appeals to me.

## 1975

**APRIL 30th** A week of strange, confusing sentiments. I worry about nuclear war, car accidents, cancer – could it be that I'm really worried about Death? Mysteriously, Jack Hargreaves has disappeared from *How* and instead of his promised opium pipe we have to settle for Bunty making a used toilet roll out of an empty washing-up bottle.

**MAY 2nd** Life is like a never-ending coil of sea-salty spume froth and dark murky deeps, oh so deep, and I but a small saline sea-worm, wriggling relentlessly hopelessly, oh please someone tell me what is the meaning, I pant, as mutilated mermaids moan. I decide to write to Aunty Maude of *Hearth and Homo* and seek her advice about this strange plurality of the senses.

# Hearth & Homo

Dear Confused,

Thank you for your letter and don't worry – Yes, it is quite normal for girls of your age to have the kind of feelings you describe. Why not join your local aerobics class or find an interesting hobby such as snail collecting? I must also recommend a mild astringent for the oily patch around the nose and chin.

Yours sincerely,

Aunty Maude

**MAY 5th** Letter from Aunty Maude by second post. I feel she could have spent more time exploring the essential dichotomy between ego and id in a sexually maturing adolescent, but there you go.

# CHAPTER

# 2½

# NO ChaPTeR

## 1975

### OCTOBER 21ST

BLEAK DAY. UNEMPLOYMENT REACHES OVER A MILLION FOR THE FIRST TIME SINCE THE WAR. BUY A FRENCH-MADE BLACK ARMBAND AND WEAR IT WITH MY SUIT. UNFORTUNATELY THERE IS A SLIGHT COLOUR CLASH.

### NOVEMBER 8TH

BARRY KEPPLE INSISTED WE GO AND SEE SOME NEW POP BAND WHO WERE PLAYING AT HIS COLLEGE. A RIGHT BLOODY MESS, BUT BOY DID THEY HAVE A WAY WITH MELODY. HOWEVER, I WAS A BIT MIFFED WHEN THEY TURNED DOWN MY REQUEST FOR KENNY'S "FANCY PANTS". WHO DO THESE "SEX PISTOLS" THINK THEY ARE - THE BAY CITY ROLLERS?

### NOVEMBER 17TH

MY BIRTHDAY, AND WHAT A DISASTER! MUM BOUGHT ME A SKINNY TIE AND A PAIR OF STRAIGHT-LEGGED JEANS, WHICH BUST THEIR ZIP THE FIRST TIME I PUT THEM ON. HAD TO RESORT TO A COUPLE OF SAFETY PINS TO HIDE MY EMBARRASSMENT, OR AT ANY RATE TO KEEP MY NOB FROM FALLING OUT. TO TOP IT ALL, I ACCIDENTALLY RIPPED THE SLEEVES OFF THE NEW SHIRT SUE GAVE ME WHILE DANCING TO A SHOWADDYWADDY DISC. WHY INTELLIGENT PEOPLE STILL BUY BRITISH IS ONE OF LIFE'S MYSTERIES.

### NOVEMBER 18TH

FASHION CRISIS DUE TO BROKEN WASHING MACHINE (BRITISH OF COURSE) SO I HAD TO GO DOWN THE HIGH STREET SHOPS WITH MY BROKEN FLIES IN FULL VIEW. ON THE WAY BACK BUMPED INTO BARRY KEPPLE WHO WAS KNOCKED OUT (NOT LITERALLY OF COURSE). "SO THE PISTOLS REALLY GOT TO YOU THEN?" HE DRAWLED IN THAT PARTICULARLY IRRITATING ACCENT HE OFTEN AFFECTS. I JUST LOOKED AT HIM IN AMAZEMENT AND WENT HOME TO WATCH SUPERSONIC.

### NOVEMBER 19TH

SAW A FASHION SPREAD IN THE NME AND THEY WERE ALL WEARING SAFETY PINS! LOOKS LIKE I'VE HIT ON SOMETHING — THIS EVENING I SHALL POLISH MY SAFETY PINS TILL THEY LOOK ALL SHINY AND SMART. CAN'T WAIT FOR THE NEXT SEX PISTOLS CONCERT.

### DECEMBER 10TH

THE COD WAR IS REALLY HOTTING UP. TODAY THE ICELANDERS FIRED AT SOME OF OUR SHIPS. I WONDER WHAT JOHNNY ROTTEN THINKS ABOUT IT? I THINK I'LL BUY AN ICELANDIC FLAG AND SEW IT ONTO THE BACK OF MY SUIT. THAT'LL REALLY GET UP EVERYONE'S NOSE.

### DECEMBER 1ST
1976

DAD HAS ORDERED ME TO STAY IN FOR THE REST OF THE WEEK — HE'S FURIOUS. WE WERE WATCHING THE TODAY PROGRAMME WITH BILL GRUNDY WHEN THE SEX PISTOLS CAME ON. THEY WERE AWESOME. THEY SWORE, DRANK BEER AND SPORTED SOME OF THE MOST REFRESHINGLY INNOVATIVE DESIGNS I'VE SEEN SINCE MUD HIT THE TOP TEN. UNFORTUNATELY, WHEN I EXPRESSED MY DESIRE TO EMULATE THEM, DAD WENT MAD AND PUT HIS FOOT THROUGH THE TELLY. NOW I WON'T BE ABLE TO WATCH TISWAS, SO I'LL HAVE EVEN MORE TIME TO PLAN THE PUNK ROCK BAND I WANT TO FORM.

## DECEMBER 3RD

I'VE CHANGED MY NAME TO JOHNNY SPASM, AND HAVE LEARNT THE E MINOR CHORD ON MY OLD BEATLE GUITAR.

## DECEMBER 10TH

PUT AN AD IN THE LEYTONSTONE GUARDIAN:

**Wanted musicians.** Ability not important. Attitude to *Starsky and Hutch* crucial.

## DECEMBER 12TH

HELD AUDITIONS FOR MY BAND TODAY. IN THE END I HIRED BARRY KEPPLE AND MRS CRANLEIGH'S TWINS, JOSH AND TOBY — BUT ONLY ON CONDITION THEY CHANGE THEIR NAMES.

## 1977  JANUARY 1ST

FIRST GIG! IT WENT REALLY WELL, ESPECIALLY THE BIT WHERE THE SCOUT MASTER ASKED US TO PLAY SOME BACKGROUND MUSIC TO PASS THE PARCEL. TODAY THE CAMDEN TOWN 11TH, TOMORROW THE MARQUEE. WE GOT PAID £5 AND AS MANY WOGGLES AS WE COULD CARRY.

## FEBRUARY 3RD

EVERYONE IN THE BAND WANTS ME TO RIP MY SUIT TO SHREDS ON STAGE. THEY SAY IT'S REALLY ANARCHIC, A DECONSTRUCTION OF THE POP IMAGE. I JUST SEE IT AS A WASTE OF 50 QUID. AGREED TO UNKNOT MY TIE BEFORE THE ENCORE. HAVE I GONE TOO FAR?

## JUNE 7TH

JUBILEE DAY. PLAYED "GOD SAVE THE QUEEN" BY THE PISTOLS ALL AFTERNOON, BUT I COULDN'T HEAR A THING; THERE WAS A STREET PARTY ON AND IT WAS SO NOISY. SOME PEOPLE HAVE NO CONSIDERATION.

## NOVEMBER 1ST

OUR FIRST SINGLE IS OUT! IT'S CALLED "BABY YOU'RE FAST, FASTER THAN PREMATURE EJACULATION" AND IS ABOUT A DEFECTIVE CHOCOLATE MACHINE ON THE UNDERGROUND.

**NEVER MIND THE BOLLOCKS**

havent Got any

## NOVEMBER 5TH

GOOD NEWS AND BAD NEWS. THE GOOD NEWS— WE FINALLY GET A REVIEW IN THE NME. THE BAD NEWS — AFTER READING IT I DECIDE TO QUIT THE MUSIC BUSINESS.

## 1979  MARCH 21ST

HAVEN'T BEEN OUT FOR FOUR MONTHS. NOW THAT I'VE LEFT THE BAND NONE OF MY OLD FRIENDS WANTS TO KNOW ME. EVEN IVAN AILMENT DIDN'T SPIT AT ME WHEN I SAW HIM DOWN THE PUB. NOW ALL I DO IS STAY IN AND READ. A LARGE PILE OF MAGAZINES IS BEGINNING TO ACCUMULATE UNDER MY BED, SOME OF THEM ARE STUCK TOGETHER. MUST DO SOMETHING ABOUT THE DAMP IN MY ROOM.

## APRIL 1ST

SAW THE JAM ON TOP OF THE POPS AND SUDDENLY MY LIFE HAS NEW MEANING.

## APRIL 2ND

WENT OUT AND BOUGHT A PARKER IN FACT I'M USING IT TO WRITE THIS DIARY

## APRIL 15T-

VISITED WOKING WITH SOME FRIENDS TO SEE THE COUNCIL HOUSE PAUL WELLER WAS BROUGHT UP IN. YOU CAN REALLY SEE THE HARSH ENVIRONMENT THAT HAS SHAPED HIS LYRICS. AFTERWARDS WENT HOME AND DRANK SOME FROTHY COFFEE IN THE PRIVACY OF MY OWN ROOM.

## MAY 15TH

FRENCH EXAM. TURNED UP IN A WHITE FRED PERRY, ORIGINAL 501's AND CERISE HUSH PUPPIES.

## MAY-16

WORE MY NEW SUNGLASSES TO THE HISTORY EXAM.

## MAY 18 TH

GEOGRAPHY, MY LAST EXAM. WORE MY BLUE MOHAIR SUIT IN CELEBRATION. HOWEVER, NOT ALLOWED TO WEAR MY PORKPIE HAT, WHICH PUT ME OFF MY STROKE A BIT

## Johnny Spasm and the Spermcounts

### THE PIT AND THE PENDULUM CLUB, PENGE, LONDON

I'M READING A COPY of T S Eliot's *The Wasteland* in the toilet of the Pit and the Pendulum, Penge; Johnny Spasm and the Spermcounts are on stage. They play and I pull the chain with one hand and hold onto my paperback with the other. The toilet noise rushes through my senses and the Spermcounts hit the first three, the only three, chords of "Doris Hare You're a Dog". A moment of beauty and revelation is reached. I walk out of the toilet and towards the stage, rubbing some rough toilet paper against my face. The friction is so perfect. Then I see the singer, the star... Johnny Spasm is wearing a Mr Byrite suit and a kipper tie. His face is clean, his barnet bequiffed. I return to the toilet with the latest Jackie Collins, lower the seat and think. I am thinking about a Mr Byrite suit. I have to get out of this place.

**Paul Maughleigh**

28

# CHAPTER THREE

## 1979-1982

### The Getting of Wisdom

## 1979

**AUGUST 29th**      London University have offered me a place on their Sanskrit and Media Studies course. Who knows? – if I work hard and play my cards right I might one day be as intelligent as Benny Green.

**SEPTEMBER 5th**      I've made out a list of the essential things I will need for my studies:

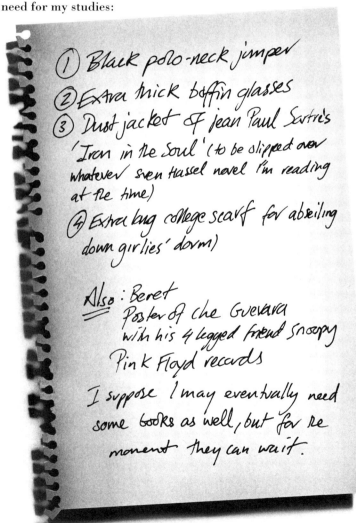

① Black polo-neck jumper
② Extra thick boffin glasses
③ Dust jacket of Jean Paul Sartre's 'Iron in the Soul' (to be slipped over whatever Sven Hassel novel I'm reading at the time)
④ Extra long college scarf for abseiling down girlies' dorm)

<u>Also</u> : Beret
Poster of Che Guevara with his 4 legged friend Snoopy
Pink Floyd records

I suppose I may eventually need some books as well, but for the moment they can wait.

**'Not just a Pretty Face'**

**OCTOBER 10th**      First day of University. A savage disappointment. There was no Free Sex, no Demos, and I actually saw someone wearing FLARES.

**OCTOBER 15th**     There comes a time in every young boy's life when he finally has to cut loose, take the plunge, let go of his mother's apron strings, and stand on his own two feet, although not necessarily in that order. That time has come for me, and at tea-time today I announced to my family that I was finally leaving the safety and creature comforts of home for the rough-and-tumble existence of a shared student house. They all tried very hard to dissuade me, but eventually after three and a half minutes of furious argument and a tear or two, mum made me a sandwich and waved me on my way.

Fresher's Week at University. It took me a couple of days to realise the point of this annual event for first-year students. The main idea seems to be to join as many student societies as possible before the bar opens, and then get absolutely pissed. That is, apart from the medical students who don't bother with the society-joining part. I also encountered the President of the Rugby Club who called me a "Southern Wanker" before grabbing my private parts and biting my face... or was it the other way around?

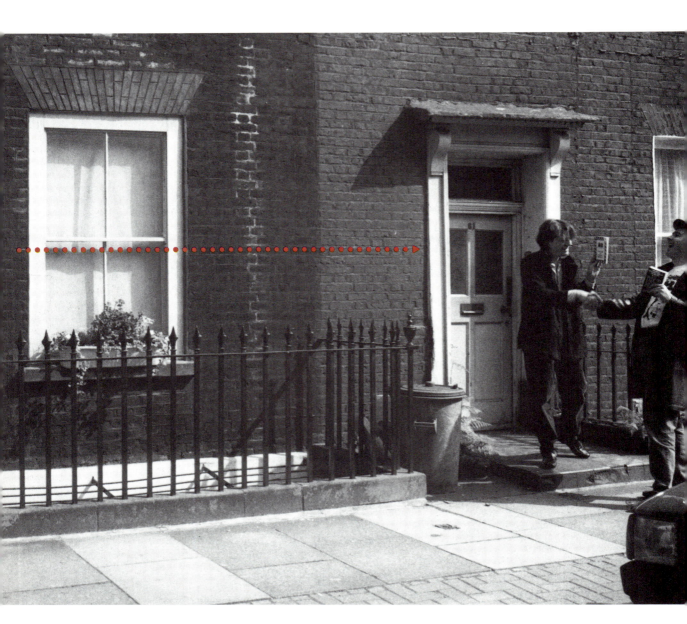

**OCTOBER 26th** Started hanging out with my beret and Sartre in the college coffee bar. All the serious types go there for a chat about the situation in Nicaragua and the latest Joy Division record. Yesterday a girl named Samantha admired my toggle.

**OCTOBER 27th** Nearly the end of Freshers' Week and I still haven't found the right society. Legalise-It-Soc certainly won my heart with their "taster" meeting, but the bloke who tried to enrol me was wearing a headband and kept calling everyone "dude". Besides, how can I be seen on demos with a man who still thinks love-beads are hip?

**OCTOBER 28th** Decided I wasn't quite ready for Feminist Bird-Watching Soc, or the Gay Love Drama Group, despite their introductory offer of a pet hamster, so in the end I plumped for the Kill The Rich Bastards (Under 21's Group). I guess everyone has a bit of rebelliousness in their system at my age, and besides, Comrade Samantha was very convincing with her skin-tight arguments.

**NOVEMBER 5th** Went to the Tory Club to heckle. Some smarmy Cabinet minister was supposed to be talking about privatisation, but all he seemed to do was stick his hand up his secretary's dress.

**NOVEMBER 15th** Went to the Labour Club to heckle. Some freckle-face Welsh nonentity was speaking. Quite interesting, actually, though I was surprised he decided to talk about pop videos rather than the future of socialism. Who *is* Tracey Ullman?

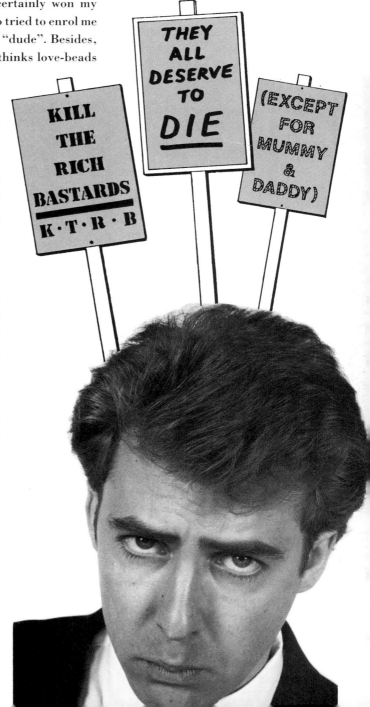

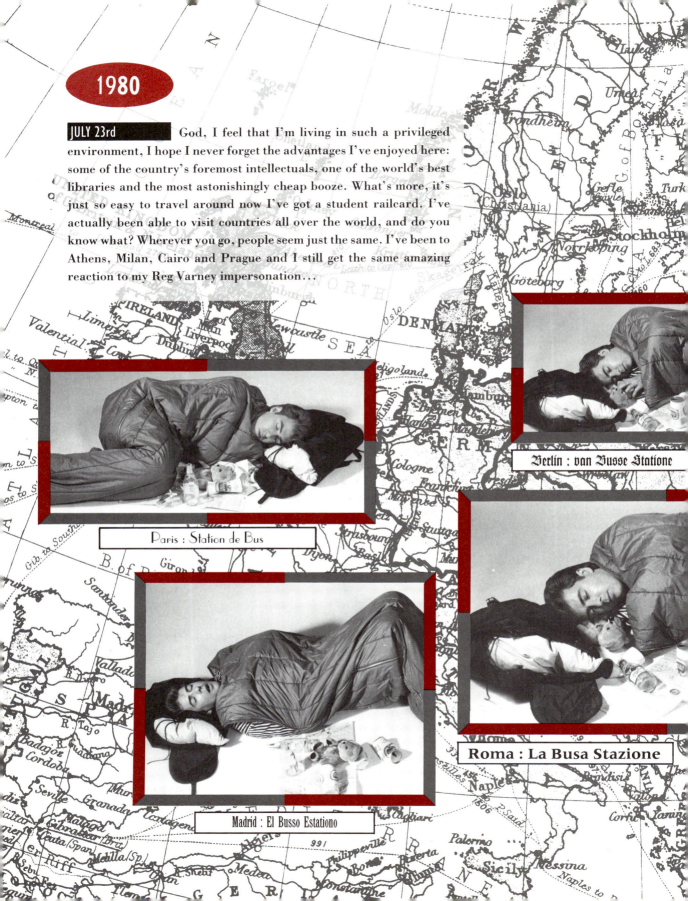

**1980**

`JULY 23rd` God, I feel that I'm living in such a privileged environment, I hope I never forget the advantages I've enjoyed here: some of the country's foremost intellectuals, one of the world's best libraries and the most astonishingly cheap booze. What's more, it's just so easy to travel around now I've got a student railcard. I've actually been able to visit countries all over the world, and do you know what? Wherever you go, people seem just the same. I've been to Athens, Milan, Cairo and Prague and I still get the same amazing reaction to my Reg Varney impersonation…

Berlin : van Busse Statione

Paris : Station de Bus

Madrid : El Busso Estationo

Roma : La Busa Stazione

**Москва: Станция Автобусов**

**OCTOBER 11th**     Another year at college and I don't think I can face up to my K.T.R.B. chums anymore. The summer camp in Salford was the last straw, I just can't keep up with all this heady socialising.

**OCTOBER 12th**     This year I decided to keep things quiet and joined Parkinson Soc: a group of people devoted to a well-known disease that appears on telly every Saturday night.

**OCTOBER 15th**     V. successful first meeting of Parkinson Soc. Had to speak for half an hour on my childhood in Barnsley.

## 1981

**OCTOBER 10th**     Can't believe it – I'm about to embark on my last year at University and I have yet to dress up in a nurse's uniform for Rag Week. That notwithstanding, I feel I have grown up a lot over the last couple of years both morally, spiritually and intellectually, to name but two. I can now have no excuse for being either apolitical or mercenary.

**OCTOBER 12th**     Joining the SDP Club has given me an idea – I'll form my own society. After all, you only need twenty members to get a £300 grant.

**OCTOBER 16th**     The Norman Scott Appreciation Society met for the first time today. We spent £4 on the ceremonial club pillow and then repaired to the Dog and Shotgun with the rest of the cash.

Seeing as exams are looming I thought I'd better start being more diligent, so instead of going to the pub I stayed in and watched some show called *3-2-1* on the telly. It's presented by a man with a twitchy hand and is almost completely unintelligible, but whoever does the voice-over announcements is FANTASTIC!

**1982**

UNIVERSITY OF LONDON EXAMINATION BOARD

BA (TWENTIETH CENTURY CLOTHES) PART II EXAMINATION 1982

STYLE AND THE RUSSIAN REVOLUTION

Tuesday 11 June: 2.30 p.m. to 5.30 p.m.

Answer THREE questions, including ONE from Section A and ONE from Section B.

### SECTION A

1. Discuss: Lenin's peaked cap – inspirational motif of the Revolution or bourgeois affectation?

2. Trotsky's glasses: pure late period John Lennon or an early example of collectivised health provision?

3. The Soviet flag: red rag to a White Army or a nice backdrop at a Spandau Ballet gig?

4. Constructivism: meeting of the industrial proletariat and art or an early graphic device in The Face magazine?

### SECTION B

1. In what sense is Celebrity Squares an empty riposte to John Reed's Ten Days That Shook The World?

2. "Bob Geldof's 'Rat Trap', a Trotskyist plea in a Stalinist world?" – Robert Maughleigh, NME. Discuss.

3. In what way was Man About The House an example of Soviet style sexual equality?

4. Were loonpants a sign of the inevitable decline of capitalism, and what would happen if they caught on in the Soviet Union?

c University of London

82/5230                    Page 1

Did my last exam today. Hooray! I think I'll go out and have a few drinks.

# CHAPTER FOUR

**1982-1984**

The Lost Years

Why I refuse to be in this book

By

# ANNE DIAMOND

1 I'm horrible 2 I'm utterly utterly despicable

3 Yuck, I'm so revolting I was almost sick just now when I thought about myself.

# CHAPTER FIVE

**1985-1986**

Fame Beckons

**JANUARY 4th** God knows where the last two years went. They just flew by. University seems a lifetime away and I still haven't realised any of my showbiz ambitions.

**JANUARY 6th** Really depressed. There I was thinking I'd really mastered voice control – acquired that deep Richard Burton-like tone, when I happened to catch *Sale of the Century* on the telly. The announcer! I'm not joking – a voice like velvet and a stage presence straight out of the Richard Wattis Drama Academy. Must remember to watch next week and practise speaking like that cove – John something or other.

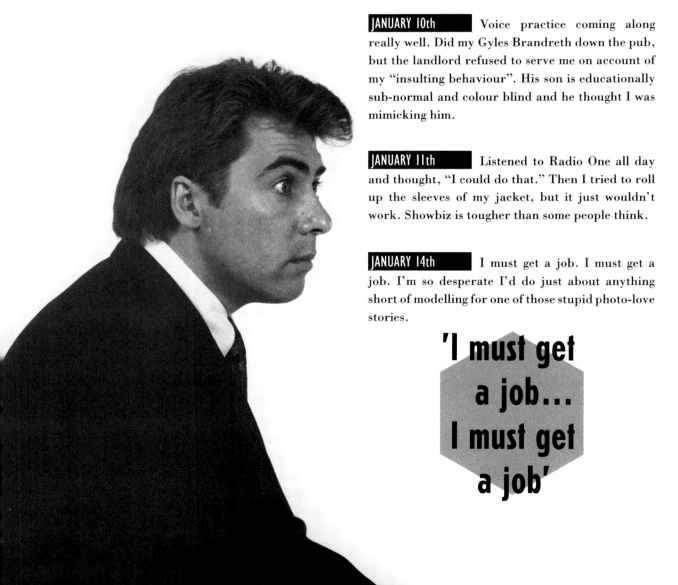

**JANUARY 10th** Voice practice coming along really well. Did my Gyles Brandreth down the pub, but the landlord refused to serve me on account of my "insulting behaviour". His son is educationally sub-normal and colour blind and he thought I was mimicking him.

**JANUARY 11th** Listened to Radio One all day and thought, "I could do that." Then I tried to roll up the sleeves of my jacket, but it just wouldn't work. Showbiz is tougher than some people think.

**JANUARY 14th** I must get a job. I must get a job. I'm so desperate I'd do just about anything short of modelling for one of those stupid photo-love stories.

'I must get a job... I must get a job'

EVENTUALLY AN AMBULANCE WAS CALLED…

Well, thanks for talking to me. I've really enjoyed it. Perhaps we can do it again sometime. Maybe I could visit you in hospital.

THE NEXT DAY JONATHAN DECIDED TO VISIT HIS NEW FRIEND IN HOSPITAL.

Life is worth living now that I have a friend. You know, in many ways I feel as if she's more than a friend. I hope she likes these flowers.

HOSPITAL

Hello. I've come to visit the girl I fell on yesterday. I think she's in this ward…

I'm terribly sorry… I'm afraid she died last night.

Dead? She can't be… there must be some mistake.

I'm sorry, Mr Ross. There was nothing we could do. But, erm… if those flowers are going spare, I'd certainly be interested!

Really? Well, in that case they're yours! I don't suppose you fancy going to the pictures tonight?

I'd love to. It's a date!

Sounds great!

I'll tell you what. My flat is near the cinema. You can pop in afterwards for a coffee.

**SEPTEMBER 12th** It's true what they say about unemployment making one apathetic and depressed. It's a struggle to rise before lunchtime and afterwards I can't get out of bed. Sometimes I watch videos all afternoon, dreaming of the day when I can afford a TV set, on other days I keep abreast of politics by drawing moustaches onto photographs of the Spanish Royal family. In the evenings I pass the time by making meaningless lists on the back of old giro envelopes and then burning them. Still, at least I haven't become peculiar.

My favourite Colours: red, blue, brown
My Second favourite Colours:
      Pink, lavender, orange
My favourite Pop star: Green

## 1986

**DECEMBER 13th** Got up late. Went down the Job Centre, still no luck, so decided to go visit mum. Picked up my dirty laundry then stopped in the news-agents. Bought a copy of **"THIS MAGAZINE CHANGES LIVES"** that great new magazine *low i-Q*. Many people regard it as an absolute BIBLE as far as Style is concerned. I felt it was embarrassingly underpriced at £27.50, but when I turned to the Classifieds at the back I saw something that was to change my life for ever...

# CARRIONI
# CABBI

*milan ● london ● new york*

# CONTENTS

**Doctor Martin Fulmer Scrote** is one of a new breed. Operating out of a small, art-deco adorned, surgery in the suburbs, Scrote is one of the top 18,000 medical practitioners in the country, a title modesty prevents him from ever using. Scrote has now forsaken the scalpel and tablet to make crucial judgements on subjects as diverse as "Footwear and the Sock", "Cutlery, Yes or No?" and the critically acclaimed "Private Posture in the Presence of a Popular Present-Day Person or Personality".

Numbered amongst his most spectacular successes to date are:

**Spandau Ballet**› It was the Doc who originally got them out of the trouser and into the skirt, then realising how stupid they looked, not to mention the fact that you could no longer see how big their "tackle" was, back into the popular trouser. The Doc had sighted Bingham's Circulation of Air Theory when promoting the skirt, a theory he later proved wrong with his creation of the ill-fated Cling-Film Loon, a trouser that never took off.

**George Michelle**› Apart from organising the change by deed poll of his surname to, initially, Malcolm and then the more popular Michael, Doctor Scrote fabricated an imaginary skin disease for George telling him that shaving would only aggravate the problem. (The Doctor had an idea that the unshaven look was going to be big but George, however, thought it untidy, preferring tennis shorts and shirt; needless to say, the Doc won the day.)

**Neil Kinnock**› The Doc talked Neil out of appearing in a particularly saucy Sam Fox video, knowing it would scupper his chances of becoming "Boss" in the party, not to mention his reconciliation attempts with Glenys. As a publicity experiment the Doc had performed some minor surgery on Neil's left knee, which the Doc knew would play up whenever he went near salt water. Kinnock had thought the Doc mad at the time. He could not see how a simple op could help in the race for votes. Doc was to prove him wrong on his very first outing to the seaside; no sooner had he and the reconciled Glenys strolled on to the beach than the "publicity" knee got to work and, splash!, in front of the whole world, he has fallen in the sea and everyone loves him.

**Sigue Sigue Sputnik**› They were told they all had a horrible bone and cartilage problem and that if they didn't keep active during the day – like maybe some kind of manual day job – their joints would seize up. Typically they all followed the Doctor's advice to the letter. Sadly this resulted in their music suffering, but as the Doc said at the time, "Better Joe Public suffers the loss of their music than they suffer the loss of mobility." When questioned about the diagnosis the Doctor would only say that it was "a very rare disease – only 1 in 1,243,001,000 people had it, and, yes, it was strange that probably the only five people in the world with it were all in the very same band, a funny thing fate."

However, it's not just celebrities who visit Scrote's surgery. A session on the good Doctor's couch has replaced a trip to the sports club or Health Farm as the fashionable way to make money and STILL feel good about yourself.

If you've got money to burn, Scrote's surgery is the place to do it. Although the Doctor is fully aware of the damage black smoke inhalation can do, he'll regularly burn people's credit cards, sovereigns, gold fillings, identity bracelets and those South African coins with the funny-sounding name. Scrote's philosophy is simple: "If your loved one suddenly takes to wearing polyester or laughing at 'Live From Jongleurs', you'd be perturbed. If you woke up one morning and discovered you were the only person on your YTS course not wearing a tea-strainer in their lapel you'd be alarmed. These are precisely the kind of modern problems I cater for." Doctor Scrote can be contacted on Isleworth 2125. Fees start at approx £15,000 or a packet of Woodies.

CLASSIC, TIMELESS, PROFOUND, THE OPPOSITE OF WHITE ... MATT BLACK IS THE COLOUR OF THE PERFECT MODERN ACCESSORY. A HEAVEN-SENT SAVIOUR FOR ALL THAT TAT YOU COLLECTED BEFORE YOU STARTED READING *LOW I-Q*, AND STOPPED WEARING SKINNY LEATHER TIES WITH MUSICAL NOTES ON THEM. MATT BLACK IS THE INSPIRATION THAT BINDS OUR AGE.

IT'S ALWAYS BEEN THE *LOW I-Q* MAXIM THAT STYLE IS INDIVIDUAL, THAT BEAUTY DOES NOT ALWAYS COME FROM POCKET-BOOKS AND THAT FAT PEOPLE SHOULD BE BANNED FROM NIGHTCLUBS. FOLLOW OUR GUIDE TO MATT BLACK AND THE WORLD OF TRUE DESIGNER LIVING WILL BE OPEN EVEN TO YOU!

**Spaghetti** » Tagliatelle verde? No grazie! Europe's two design capitals, Italy and Denmark, have joined forces to produce this glamorous licorice-flavour spaghetti. And if you accidentally leave it sizzling in the pan for three hours nobody will even notice. Per piacere! £5.00 per lb.

**Toothpaste** » Style hits pharmaceuticals! And not only does it look good, but it tastes good too. This Japanese sushi-flavour toothpaste looks good on the bathroom shelf and keeps teeth sparkling grey. £8.99.

**Pictures** » Is it art or just a load of horrible colours? Whether it's an old family photo or a Chagall lithograph, these stylish black picture screens conceal any picture in any frame. From £65.95.

**Golf ball** » A stupid game played by middle-aged men in tartan trousers – n'est-ce pas? So why bother with a ball you can really use when this clever fibre-glass replica says both 'Hello Fashion' and 'Goodbye golf' at the same time?

**Plants** » For centuries people have had to put up with plants which were available only in green, or, even worse, which sometimes bore brightly coloured flowers. But Black Gardens of Chelsea have now come up with a clever scorching technique which enables you to have gardens without the gaudiness. From £200.

**Before**      **After**

**Cat** » You're too fond of your pussy to have it destroyed, but it just doesn't blend with the decor? Just out, this new matt-black spray makes moggy look like new and saves your face as well as vet bills. £45.00.

**Light bulb** » Still got a white light bulb, Grandad? Never fear — you can now combine 40's Retro and 80's cool with this 60-watt 'Matt Blackout'. But don't forget to stock up on candles! £12.25.

**Milk Bottle** » Gotta lotta bottle? Thenna throwa away youra olda pintas, dickheadas and getta theesa!

49

# CLUB

**Peasants, industrial proletariat and aristocracy go back to the future at edinburgh's latest club**

**I'm standing in the middle of Edinburgh's most fashionable nightclub talking to Jeff.**

Jeff is wearing cotton cossack trousers, a satin waistcoat and Wellington boots. He's talking to me about the 1832 Reform Bill. "Reform is one thing," he says pausing to take some snuff, "but we shouldn't go too far. Look at the peasants." He points an ivory-topped cane towards a group of people wearing rough hessian outer-garments, they are huddled around one pint of lager and a packet of crisps. "They've seen what's happened in France and by jove they're after revolution here as well."

In dark, distant corners of this disused public sewer be-chained Tolpuddle Martyrs carry the act of penal servitude well beyond the imagination of their 1834 inspiration, whilst Mr Bumble lookalikes lead young Oliver Twists in faithful homage to the Poor Law Amendment Act. Over the sound system comes the voice of Ms Kylie Minogue. This is Club 1830, the scene that's taken the whole of Scotland by storm, and an eclectic bunch of Edinburgh's finest back, for one night a week, to the 1830's.

# 1830

Tarquin Curtis, a 21-year-old fashion student is the inspiration behind this nocturnal trip into nostalgia.

"We had nowhere to go," he says. "The 1970's revival was played out, the 60's revival was going nowhere fast, we were desperate. Some of us took a look at the 1930's, but the Jarrow March was terribly unstylish.

"It had to be the 1830's, it had everything: the discipline of the Poor Law, the pomp and splendour of Queen Victoria's Coronation, the thrill of quashing the Chartist movement, not to mention leg-of-mutton sleeves."

Tarquin is busy organising Club 1830's biggest event yet: a club-night on a train running along the original Stockton to Darlington railway line. Purists point out that the Stockton-Darlington railway line was first used by trains in 1825, but Tarquin is unrepentant. "That's not important," he says, swatting a workhouse girl with his riding crop. "It's the spirit that matters and the 1830's were a great period of development on the railways. They had such great ideas, like First, Second and THIRD class compartments. You knew where your place was in those days."

As Tarquin moves off to instruct some poorer members of his ensemble to pick oakum, a spinning prison-style treadmill descends to the dance floor and young girls, in bloomers and corsets, begin working their way up the treadmill to the sound of Madonna.

story: draylon loons / illustrations: boz

## 1830's Sayings

Yo poor boy
Please sir, can I have some more?
Lancashire cotton mills? – loadsamoney

## 1830's Places

The open sewer, Boggleside, Lancs – fine repository of early cholera germs.
E. Chadwick Memorial Park, Hovis Street, Holmfirth, Yorks – early example of the two-tier toilet facilities available in Victorian parks. Conveniences are marked 'Rich' (respectable urinal, seat on toilet, words of national anthem engraved in the marble floor) and 'Poor' (four-foot trench hidden from view behind the trees).
YTS Training Centre, Skelmersdale – splendid revival of the spirit of the Poor Law.
The Midden, Industrial Street, East London – affectionately known by locals as 'the shithole'.

## 1830's Fashion Accessories

Begging bowl
Leg irons
Copy of *Chartism Today* ostentatiously hanging out of back pocket
Victorian fireplace with integral chimney sweep

# C L A S S I F I E D

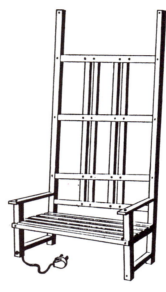

# CHAPTER SIX

## 1987

### The Champion of Chat

**JANUARY 2nd** Can't believe I've actually got the job. Me! On television! They're all such a nice bunch of people as well. Not only are they buying me a couple of new suits but they've even insisted on paying for some specialist beauty treatment. What a start to 1987!

**JANUARY 5th**

Channel Four sent me to see the famous plastic surgeon Dr Scrote at his famous Wigmore St Emporium. Such a nice man (pity about the alopecia) – he seemed really enthusiastic and hopeful that he could help me get a look that will take me to The Top. Today I also went for my first lesson at the Dick Van Dyke Academy of Elocution. They've got such famous alumni as Frank Muir, Janet Street-Porter and Danny Baker (aka Viscount Stanmore). I was supposed to join the class learning to drop their aitches, but I got talking to Ben Elton in the foyer and by the time I went to register all they had left was double-u's. Never mind, it seems like a nice bunch of people although that Roy Jenkins is a real attention-seeker.

## Dick Van Dyke Academy

### of Elocution

# SCROTE

Proposal from Dr Scrote.

To: Jonathan Ross.

From: Dr Martin Scrote, M.D., M.R.C.S.,
(expelled '76 but reinstated in '84)

Dear Jon Jon,
         Re; making you look 'the part', I carn't see there
being any problems at all. In fact, truth be known, Im
champing at the bit to get started. Bugger me, it's been
a ges since I've done any of that sort of work, not since
Susan Hampshire had her 'George Formby' done and, sod it,
if thats not going back a bit I don't know what is. But
don't worry, once I get started It'll soon come back to me.
         As regards payment for the job, I'll get in touch
with your mum, sort something out with her. I'm sure we can
come to some kind of 'mutual arrangement', heck, we don't
need to be messing with cash for an op' as simple as the
one yo ur after.
         All I will ask you to do however, is remember it's
pro bably going to be a nat's painful, so maybe think
about getting pissed out of your head beforehand, most
doctors I know recommend the lighter family of spirits for
the job.
         Anyway must dash, things to do, you know ho w it is.
Oh, and tell yo ur Mum I'll be in touch, failing that she
knows where to find me.
         Your do cto r,

# ALL MY OWN WORK

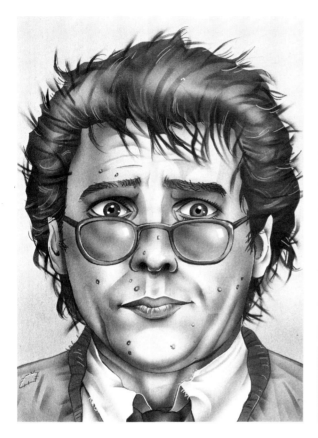 

Patient in need of minor refirbishment with particular emphasis to the nose (bridge and nostril), mouth, ear, earlobe, forehead, cheek, chin, teeth, hair line and eyebrow. I am reluctant to do anything with the eyes as I know bugger all all about them (anyway they're all squashy and difficult to ho ld). Consequently I will attempt to conduct the whole operation without disturbing the patient's funny glasses.

As you can see pro gress has been made in what I can only hope and prey is the right direction, these things are so hard to tell at this stage - even for me and I'm a Doctor! Not everything went according to plan. For o ne, I'd co mpleatly forgotten about my planned ho liday travelling the length of the Severn Valley Railway, meaning I had to leave the patient shortly after the first few incisions. This was rather a shame as it was going quite well. For two, when I got back so me callous bastard had nicked his glasses, some people.

Really making progress, had to remove quite
a bit of yucky stuff from just behind his
face. Thought I'd pop it in a yoghurt carton
for safe kepping - I've an idea I might need
it later on, if not the cat can have it. Bit
wo rried about the skin, it seems to get
lighter and darker as often as the days.
Decided to go with the pointy nose as it's
always popular and seems to photograph well
- just look at Petula Clark.

I think I might have gotten a bit too heavy
handed , although someone did remark how
funny he looked and lets face it (ha, ha,)
as they say, 'any criticism is good criticism'.
At this stage, to me, he's looking a bit like
that animal from that film about a kids
garden and his bike and how they all go to a
party but carn't get home. Or am I thinking
of Liz Taylor? Anyway, still not quite right.

EASTBURY

I think I might have cracked it. The whacky
hair was wrong, I admit that now. As for
the Pet Clark nose, how stupid of me. I've
adopted a more slap dash approach to my work
and I think it's paying off. He's relly
begining to  look like something special,
or at least... like something. The lighter
hair, the fuller face are the sort of things
I thought I co uld never achieve. What I
really need now is a bit of loose skin, that
always goes down well, but where to find it?
Eureka! That's it! The yucky stuff in the
yoghurt carton, I tell you some things really
are heaven sent - now where's that bloody cat.

Words fail me. Very rarely can a Doctor turn
round and say, "it's been a 100% success".
That sort of moment o nly happens once in a
lifetime, and it's actually happened to  me.
Yes, about three years ago after a brilliant
ear syringing, I loo ked at the little kid
sitting there, water and wax all down his
shirt, tears in the little fellas eyes, and
I said, "kid, it's been a 100% success".
Sadly I cannot say that of, what was to all
intents and purposes, a simple 'Star Quality'
tuck and stitch. Don't get me wrong, this ones
go ing straight to the top, there's just a few
niggling bits that, I'm sure, even God himself
would have to say, "sod it, that's the best I
can do", and I'm inclined to agree with him.

**JANUARY 12th** Today the team and I spent a long time deciding on exactly the right mix for this all-important maiden programme. In the end we settled on the idea of having one American film actor, one British film actor, a pop singer, and a token Bimbo. In enthusiastic mood, I wrote to all concerned.

**JANUARY 14th** Slight setback today. This morning's post brought letters of regret from three of the celebrities we'd asked to appear. No news from the pop singer.

**JANUARY 16th** Oh dear, nobody seems to be able to be in the first episode. I suppose it's not really surprising when you consider they're such big stars. We were fools only to give them six months' notice. Still, I refuse to be downhearted.

**JANUARY 18th** I knew it! We've finally got a load of acceptances. They're all really keen too.

**JANUARY 20th** The pop singer finally got in touch today. It turns out she will be available on the day we want. I write back, politely declining. If we have someone called Madonna on the show people might think it was a religious programme and that wouldn't help the ratings much, would it? Anyway, Keith's cousin Toni has offered to do the music slot and she's got Grade Six clarinet.

**JANUARY 21st** All in all, I think we've done very well. For a first show I think it's a cracking line-up.

**ARTHUR STEPHENS**... a gardener from Hove

**DEREK LUBBOCK**... the producer's brother

**THALIA KERSHAW**... Channel Four make-up girl

**PHILIOS NIARCHOS**... a kebab-shop owner near Harry Enfield's house

Dear Jonathan,
Thankyou for inviting me on your show. I shan't be able to make the 15th as I will be tidying my room.

Clint

(Clint Eastwood)

*Babcock and Pritt*
**SOLICITORS**

Dear Jonathan Ross,

My client has requested me to instigate proceedings against you for harassment, should there be any further unsolicited mail from you in future. My client is a deeply private person who shuns publicity of any kind.

Yours,

Babcock and Pritt
(Solicitors for Ms Cynthia Payne)

Piss off
John gielgud

# *John* "DAMBUSTERS" *Benson*

## HERE'S ONE BENSON
*who's definitely Kingsize!!!*

*John is a Leo and keeps fit by racing pet hamsters around his Mayfair penthouse apartment. Not the usual kind of hobby for a continuity announcer, but we bet there's a few fillies out there in TV-land who'd like to horse around with John's rodents!!!*

**JANUARY 25th** The most exciting thing yet happened today. I got A MANAGER. Since Channel 4 have only paid me a week's wages so far, I couldn't even offer him much of a financial incentive, but he's kindly offered to let me pay him over the next ten years. It's just like being a pop star, only without the money obviously... or the drugs... or the girls... or the music for that matter, and of course I'm not famous like a pop star would be, but otherwise it's virtually identical. Gary, as his friends call him, admitted to me that he is an absolute genius, and I'm looking forward to a long and happy association.

**FEBRUARY 1st** I can't believe it – today I actually get the chance to meet Shirley Cheriton – you know, the one in *EastEnders* who used to play the woman who worked in a bank and went out with the Scottish bloke who was hit by a lorry. Anyway, last week someone rang Gary and invited me to come and open a supermarket in Croydon. Me! Well, for a while I was a bit nervous about doing it. Apart from anything else I'm very ignorant about tinned goods and things like that and I was worried that I might not be able to answer some of the shoppers' questions. But when I found out Shirley was doing it as well I said yes immediately. After all – chances like this don't come twice in a lifetime.

**FEBRUARY 5th** Someone in the office asked me if I'd ever tried cocaine. Deep down I know if I ever tried cocaine it would ruin my life. It would make me lose weight. It would cost me a **"COCAINE"** fortune. In the end I'd probably have to give up work and live in a Swiss sanatorium where I'd write my memoirs and make back all the money I'd spent on cocaine in the first place – I wonder where I could get some?

**"My first fan letter"** It's so exciting – today I got not one, but three letters. I suppose that's the weird and wonderful magic of television – when you're in front of the camera you feel like you're alone, but all the time there are literally hundreds of people watching.

DEAR JOHNATHON ROSS,

You have a sick and perverted mind the things you said abour our beloved ROYAL FAMILY AND especialy are QUEEN'S husband prince PHilip MADE me boil. I Hope you die in terrible PAIN

yours A Christian

P.S. Coud you please SEND ME A SKINY PHOTOGRAPH

Dear Jonny,
Please could you write to me and tell me what Phillip Schofield's really like? I think he's dead fit and would also like his autograph.
Yours
Brigitte Nielsen

Dear Jon, I enjoyed your performance on last week's edition of The Last Resort immensely. You have great flair for relaxed conversation, and you managed to appear witty, urbane and charming all at the same time. I have no doubt that with a talent like yours you will continue to delight audiences all over Britain, and eventually all over the world.
see you tommorow tea-time
love Dad
P.S Don't forget to bring the £15 you owe me

**MAY 12th**     Dear Diary, I hope that years from now when I am rich and famous no one ever discovers these shameful photographs and publishes them in a book, as it would be certain to ruin my career.

**MAY 13th** OK, so we all make mistakes when we're young. I had a Rod Stewart haircut, Jesus said he was the lamb of God – is that any reason to crucify a guy?

It's so EXCITING! – tomorrow I'm going to my very first showbiz dinner because apparently I've been nominated for a Radio Advertisement award. I'm in a stiff category – "Best impersonation of Charles Hawtrey in a Surgical Appliance Ad", but you can always dream.

**SEPTEMBER 27th** Had a restless night but managed to control myself by the time I got to the George Formby Memorial Hall. Being a newcomer to these events, I was placed at a table right at the back of the banqueting suite next to an extra from the People's Court. It was all I could do to stop staring in downright amazement at the faces of the people on the top table. The pecking order went something like this:

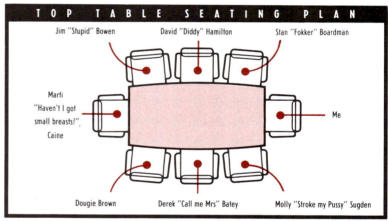

TOP TABLE SEATING PLAN

Jim "Stupid" Bowen — David "Diddy" Hamilton — Stan "Fokker" Boardman

Marti "Haven't I got small breasts?" Caine — Me

Dougie Brown — Derek "Call me Mrs" Batey — Molly "Stroke my Pussy" Sugden

To top it all, the guest speaker was none other than the great Yorkshire comedian Charlie Williams! After Charlie's hilarious speech it was time for him to give the awards out. I'm not joking, but when he mentioned my name I nearly fainted! My first year in showbiz and already I'd won an Aspel! I tried hard but I couldn't stop myself crying. It all came flooding back, those early tap-dancing lessons in Walthamstow, the first time I saw Michael Miles on *Double Your Money*, trying on mother's underwear when she was down at Tesco's – I finally understood what all that early preparation had been for. I went into my acceptance speech in a dream – luckily I had prepared a strikingly original one – I thanked my mum, my dad, everyone who voted for me, and my manicurist, and finished off with a joke about Des O'Connor. By the time I got back to my seat half the cast of *Emmerdale Farm* were calling me "Darling", and one of Larry Grayson's golfing chums had invited me to a Lodge meeting. I'm so happy.

# CHAPTER SEVEN

**1988**

## King of the Box

## 'The price of Fame'

**FEBRUARY 11th** Annoying phonecall from some guy wanting a handout. It's unbelievable! The second you appear on TV every jerk around imagines you're swimming in money.

**FEBRUARY 12th** A pleasant day, spent lounging around my new pool. Must remember to speak to my decorators about the gold and onyx taps on my jacuzzi. I really think they're much too pretentious – anyway, I always think gold looks so sweet and simple on its own.

**FEBRUARY 13th** Went to my manager's office this morning to sort out my endorsements for the next six months. He handed me a list of about a hundred products and at the bottom I wrote "These are really great products. I love them. Thanks for the dosh, Jonathan Ross." It's a tough life being a major celeb...

**FEBRUARY 14th** Valentine's Day. This year all the girlies too overawed even to send me cards anonymously. Another phonecall from the same guy begging for a loan to pay his electricity bill. Bloody cheek.

**FEBRUARY 15th** My manager rang up about some record they want me to do. The deal goes like this: I have to pick my favourite celebrity and sing a few of their ditties and in exchange the record company give me a holiday for two in the Caribbean and a ten-second peep at Cleo Rocca's knickers. Not bad, eh! There was something in the contract that worried me – something about the record company owning me and all my children for twenty years, but Gary says it's just a formality and I can ignore it. It's so good to have a manager you can trust.

**FEBRUARY 16th** Fame really does have its price. I told the guy if he called me once more I'd have to call the police. He said he was going to tell mum what a mean and nasty brother I'd become. He doesn't scare me anymore. Not now I've got my own bodyguards, anyway.

# Jonny Sings Frankie

*Salute!*

*Oh No Missus No*

*Titter Ye Not!!!*

*Francis, Call Me Francis...*

*My Kind of Toga*

*I've Been Caught by the Trinobantes*

*and many many more!!!!!!!*

Now, by popular request,
two great artists
are brought together
on one album!!!

ONLY 35p

# 'Celebs 'n' Me'

Had the first guest meeting of the new series with the *Last Resort* team of researchers. I expect lots of people spend hours wondering how we at *The Last Resort* get our guests. And no doubt they imagine that all the really famous and interesting people are queueing up to be interviewed by me. Astonishingly enough this is not always the case. Sometimes I have to give them money or even grant them sexual favours before they'll agree to appear on the show. Naturally I'm a bit fussy about who I give my money to, so I've instituted a system that whenever a celebrity name comes up in the office, the team run it past me and grade the person according to my response. All potential guests, therefore, fall into one of the four categories I have devised: And to make it even simpler, each of these is represented by a single symbol:

### Yes Please!

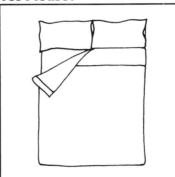

### No Thank You!

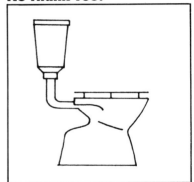

### Only If We're Desperate...

### Are They Still Alive?

Of course, in the unforgettable words of Andy Warhol, "Everyone is famous for twenty-five minutes", and celebrities who once held pride of place on our bedroom walls and the front pages of our tabloids have faded into silence and semi-obscurity. What we want to know is: where are they now? To this end we have also established a special research team to track down individuals such as the following: ▶

From researchers to JR.
Suggested guests for The Last Resort.

*must be dead?*

Jeffrey Archer

Renee Arnoux

Dan Ackroyd

Anthony Blunt *Dead*

Ronnie Barker

Anthony Burgess

Jon Cassavetes

Michael Caine

→ Archbishop of Canterbury

Carl Davis

Lord Denning *Nearly dead*

The Grateful Dead *Dead?*

Clint Eastwood

John Erlichman

Kenny Everett

✓✓✓✓ Michael Fish

Sarah Ferguson

Dawn French

Mikhail Gorbachev

Bruce Grobbelaar

*Do me a favour!* Barry Gibb

Darryl Hannah

Max Headroom *Obviously dead*

Barbara Hershey

*Dead No! Fictional*

Mother Hubbard

Ralph Halpern

Elton John

Michael Jackson

Jesse Jackson

Rabbi Jacobovits

Kris Kristofferson

The Dead Kennedys *Dead?*

Edward Kennedy *Alive*

Jimmy (Konnors) *Stop trying to fill up the K's*

Linda Lovelace

Lord Lucan (960 4770)

Red Leicester *where did you get this number*

Ivan Lendl

Freddie Mercury

Patrick Moore

Minnie the Moocher *please please please*

Paul Newman

Madonna

Nanette Newman

Gary Numan

Tom Okker *a total nonentity*

Captain Oates *Missing possibly dead*

Felix Oistrakh

*This is a cheese not a guest*

*Too many Newmans*

Oscar Peterson

Sean Penn

Itzhak Perlman *No such person*

Jon Pertwee

Picasso *Dead*

Ronald Reagan *Deadish*

Jan Ravens *who?*

Griff Rhys Jones

Peter Rabbit *oh really*

Sting *Too obvious*

Jonathan Ross

Mark Spitz

The Specials *Split*

Terence Stamp

Daley Thompson

Donald Trump

Margaret Thatcher *Not together*

Arthur Scargill

U Thant

Dick Van Dyke

Vorster

Kaiser Wilhelm

Andy Williams

Barnes Wallace

*Come off it who are you trying to kid*

*FOR CHRIST'S SAKE THESE PEOPLE ARE ALL DEAD IMBECILE!!*

*There are far too many dead people on this list. Why can't I have guests like Mick Robertson, Bobby Bennett, or Flipper on the show? Where are they now?*

● **Roy North** Soared to fame as chirpy knockabout presenter of *Basil Brush Show* and *Get It Together*. Fell from grace when it was discovered that these were a front for covert arms smuggling op. to Nicaraguan contras. Last seen in Washington DC.

● **Richard Bradford** Left *Man in a Suitcase* series in 1968 to undergo plastic surgery to remove cigarette from upper lip. Recently has suffered from weight problem though said to be planning comeback series — *Man in a Very Large Trunk*.

● **Flipper** Left series in mid 70's because he felt he was being typecast as the lovable dolphin. Eventually landed lead in off-Broadway production of *The Importance of Being Earnest*. Unfortunately dried out and died during second act.

● **Bobby Bennett** At end of *Junior Showtime* contract in 1973 reverted to former profession of mercenary soldier. Has survived spells in Angola, Beirut and Namibia. Channel 4 currently at preproduction stage of his own programme *Blade Death* — a dirty tricks survival show for five- to eight-year-olds.

● **Mick Robertson aka Brian May aka Kevin Keegan** Renaissance man — almost impossible to predict where he'll turn up next. Rumoured to be currently working as Libyan President.

**MARCH 3rd** Do I really need musical guests on the show? I could knock off a few numbers myself, I'm sure my public would appreciate that, rather than the type of overpaid teenager we're hiring at the moment. Come to that, why do we need a band? I've never forgotten how to play the spoons and you don't get much of that on TV these days, do you?

**MARCH 4th** So what's so great about John Benson anyway? I could announce myself, it's not too difficult and we could have the same speech every week: "Now live from London it's *The Last Resort* with Jonathan Ross, with singing from Jonathan Ross, spoon-playing from Jonathan Ross, guest star JR, variety..." Variety? We'll put a stop to that right away. I didn't save up my pocket money for an Ali Bongo Magic Kit to waste an opportunity like this.

**MARCH 5th** Why do people say I'm getting big-headed? I don't think my plan for a one-man opera is that outrageous.

**MARCH 6th** Rang up Aspel today and asked him why he was dragging his feet over the big red book.

**MARCH 7th** Sacked my PR; if Michael Jackson can get on the cover of *Time* and *Newsweek*, why am I stuck with *Tailors and Tailoring?*

**MARCH 9th** Sacked my girlfriend. You've gotta work hard to earn the title 'Jonathan Ross's piece of rumpy pumpy'; she seemed to think it was all to do with love or something.

**MARCH 10th** All I'm faced with is mediocrity, drudgery. Did Cecil B deMille have to knot his own tie? Did Shakespeare write his own cheques? Have you ever heard of Bernard Breslaw answering his own phonecalls? Of course not – they were geniuses. But me, what recognition do I get from the common people: "Oi, baggy pants, you can't roll your r's," that's what. Yeah, very funny. Genius is a beautiful thing. Genius ignored is shameful.

By
# BEN ELTON

**1** Be in this book? How many black people did Jonathan ask
to be in it? And what about women? How come *The Last
Resort* is always hosted by a man? Whoops bit of politics
there — well that went down like a pork chop in a synagogue.
Whoops bit of satire there . . . No don't laugh — oh you
didn't, never mind, carry on . . .

# How To Be Incredibly witty

**APRIL 2nd** People are always coming up to me in the street and saying, "Jonathan — you must be one of the wittiest people on television today. How do you *do* it? " It's not that I'm trying to be modest, but I always reply, "I don't know — I guess I'm just cleverer than all of you."

Here is an excerpt from one of my favourite scripts providing perhaps the best example of the dazzling wit and sizzling repartee that has made *The Last Resort* the resounding success it is.

## Last Resort: Episode 46

**1** JOHN BENSON'S voice: And now, live from London, it's *The Last Resort*, with the handsome champion of chat himself — Mr Jonathan Ross!

*Enter Jonathan. He is his usual cool, handsome, debonair self.* ▶

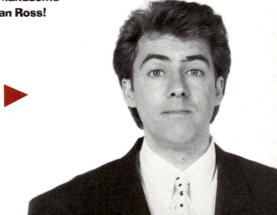

**2** JONATHAN: Hello and welcome once again to *The Last Resort;* on tonight's show we'll be talking to an American film director, we'll be having a look at some of the latest Paris fashions, we've got music, and I'll be talking to a pretty actress. But first — let's have a word with our resident band — Steve Nieve and the Playboys.

Jonathan strolls over to band, displaying new Armani suit to greatest advantage.

**3** JONATHAN: Hello, Steve.

**4** STEVE: Hello, Jonathan.

**5** JONATHAN: Hello, Pete.

**6** PETE: Hello, Jonathan.

**7** JONATHAN: Hello Steve hello JJ

**8** STEVE L AND J.J: Hi, Jonathan. How's it going?

Jonathan winks engagingly at the audience.

**9** JONATHAN: Great guys — hey Steve, have you ever wondered why John Benson spends so much time in Boots?

**10** STEVE: Boots? Do you mean those leather things you wear on your feet?

**11** JONATHAN: No, silly, I mean Boots the Chemist. Whenever I see John Benson he's either just been to Boots, just going to Boots or he's actually in Boots.

**12** STEVE: Well, that's certainly very strange, Jonathan. What do you think he's doing there?

**13** JONATHAN: I think he's probably buying lots and lots of Durex!!!

PAUSE FOR HUGE LAUGH.

So there you have it, the kind of witty, clever humour you can expect to find on any TV programme I associate myself with.

**APRIL 16th**     Went to a party for Eddie Murphy. Wanted to ask him if he'd seen my show and if he realised I was the biggest TV star in Britain, but he was surrounded by minders. His loss, not mine.

**APRIL 17th**     Rang up my manager to see if he could fix me up with a minder. He said that Ollie Reed was off-loading a job lot at quite reasonable prices.

**APRIL 20th**     Met Gnasher, my first minder, and the finest specimen of manhood to stand 5ft 2in in his socks. Had a brief chat with Gnasher about his duties, but he had to leave as his back was playing up.

**APRIL 21st**     Gnasher not at work today, he sprained his wrist doing the washing-up. Sent him some flowers.

**APRIL 22nd**     Gnasher really is a very sweet fellow. There we were watching a video of last week's show (something we do first thing every morning) when Gnasher just burst into tears. "Mr Ross, you're so kind," he said from behind a Scottie. "You treat your guests with such charm and you're kind to me as well." I ask you, has a man ever had such a devoted minder? Gave Gnasher the rest of the day off, all that crying had given him such a bad headache.

**APRIL 23rd**     Gnasher really is coming on. He's turning up to work on time and has already overcome his fear of my pet kitty, Pussy-kins.

**APRIL 24th**     Got a letter out of the blue from Eddie Murphy – very strange:

   "Dear Mr Joss," it said. "Thank you for the crumpled piece of paper you thrust into my hand at the Savoy. I wish you well in your quest for a career."

**MAY 3rd**     Am beginning to astound even myself with the enormity of my talent. Like Margot Fonteyn, Yehudi Menuhin or Rolf Harris, the true token of a professional is in making what is extremely difficult look ridiculously simple and painless. No doubt many imagine that my job as a chat-show host is easy. And how wrong they are! Anyone who saw the backstage working of an episode of *The Last Resort* would realise there is far more to doing my job than meets the eye.

# BEHIND THE SCENES AT THE LAST RESORT

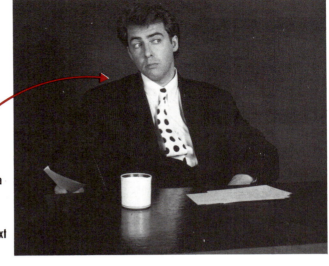

Jonathan cracks a few spontaneous gags as he introduces his next guest.

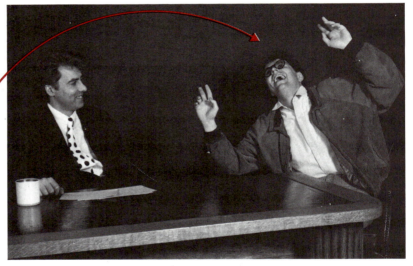

Jonathan's wit makes the guest scream with laughter.

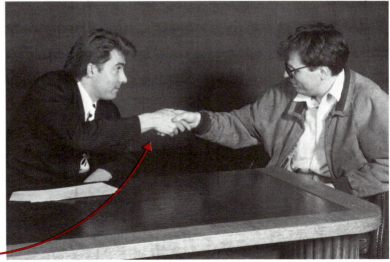

Jonathan thanks his guest.

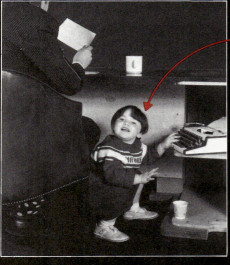

Hand-picked dwarf scriptwriters are always ready to help out with a joke.

Specially trained Last Resort prodders find the guest's funny-bone with their sharp sticks.

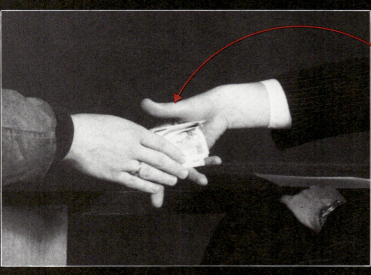

Another satisfied customer.

**MAY 19th** Woke up in a cold sweat. I'd had it again. It's the same dream I have before every show. There's a guest sitting next to me. I'm sure he's someone famous. But I can't remember who he is or what he does for a living. Maybe he's the leader of the SLD. Maybe he's the drummer from Bros. Maybe he's...oh no, oh no! I've got to start talking now!!

# *"It's the same dream I have before every show"*

**JR:** Welcome. Great to have you on the show.

**POPE:** Bless you my son.

**JR:** I haven't sneezed yet.

**POPE:** What?

**JR:** (Under his breath)
*Think, Johnny, think. He called you "My son".
Maybe he's a lovable cockney actor. Of
course! It's him!* So, Dennis, what was it like
working with George Cole on 'Minder'?

**POPE:** Please, who is George Cole?

**JR:** Ha ha ha ha. Forgotten already, eh? *For god's*

*sake look at that gear... the hat...*
Listen, I'd love to meet your tailor. What's he
on exactly?

**POPE:** I am not understanding.

**JR:** Look, tell me, er...

**POPE:** Karol.

**JR:** (*At last!*) Tell me, Carol, how long have you
been a woman?

**POPE:** Zle sie czuje! Prosze zdjac spodnie.

**Audience pelt JR with Mike Smith badges**

# The Birds, the Bees Jonathan Ross & me

I can remember as clear as day when Johnny first asked me about the birds and the bees. I took a deep breath and then his hand — something that doctors all over the world do to reassure people — and just smiled. Holding it firmly, I led him over to an array of glass cabinets that made for a permanent, informative visual display in my surgery. Johnny's eyes lit up, he had the look of someone about to discover the meaning of life or, more importantly, the reason Christopher Biggins is a household name (I must just add that Chris was another fresh-faced lad who had asked me the same question only a few days before. To him I had lied, saying, in a pathetic half-Pakistani and half-not-Pakistani voice, "Go away and eat a lot." The rest as they say…).

Johnny's eyes were right out on the biggest stalks I have ever seen as we approached the impressive display cases that were to explain all. Once again he cleared his throat using the rectum inspection tube he'd purchased from me some months earlier, and asked, "So Doc, what is it with all this Birds and Bees stuff anyway!"

"It's to do with obsession and intrigue, with beauty and nature, with things being at one with each other," I replied.

Johnny seemed not quite to grasp what I was drivelling on about and in a half-frustrated and therefore half-not-frustrated voice inquired again, this time using notably fewer words.

"What's it all about Scrota," he said. "Come on, give."

It was at that moment I realised his future, his career, would see him ambling down some kind of public relations path — how right I proved to be.

"You want to know about the Birds and the Bees!" I said in a carrot-dangly way.

"Yes. Course I bloody do!" he replied, this time his face pressed hard up against one of the larger display cabinets.

"Well, it's quite simple," I said, "you see, I'm into taxidermy and these birds and bees you see before you are the birds and bees I've collected and mounted in settings similar to their natural habitat. They have all been stuffed by my own fair hand in this very surgery."

Johnny's face gradually lightened and a smile the like of which I'd never seen before crept across his face. He suddenly acquired the air of someone who had just discovered the meaning of life or who had just realised that because Christopher Biggins was fat and effeminate, he was bound to be popular.

"I see," he said, "I see it all now, these are just animals and insects that you've killed, disembowelled and stuffed with sawdust."

Suddenly you could hear the joy in his thin voice.

"Yes. You see, I'm a Doctor," I said. "Look, I've got all the right tools to do it." I opened one of my many filing cabinets and proudly displayed an array of surgical tools all arranged alphabetically. Johnny sat on a very small footstool and contemplated what he had just learnt. I took the opportunity to roll a cigarette. Suddenly he turned towards me and with that familiar blank expression, an expression that was to become his passport through life, said, "But Doctor, what about shagging!"

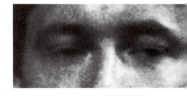

by Dr Scrote

# Relative Values

Mrs Nora Ross is 63 and lives on the Sir Stafford Cripps estate in Lower Clapton, East London, with her cat, Letterman

## NORA ROSS

"As a mother, you're always worrying about your children. I gave in to every one of Jon Jon's wishes when he was growing up: letting him wear a pink frock for his fifteenth birthday, allowing him to pour acid on my face when I bought him a chemistry set, pretending I was the char-lady when his friends came round. It was great fun.

"Jonathan was always very ambitious. When he was two, he used to look out of the front window, clench his chubby little hands and say, 'One day I'll leave this dump behind, tell the press I was brought up in an orphanage and finally rid myself of this creepy family.' He was always playing little jokes like that.

"Even though he's got a busy schedule now he always thinks of me. How many mothers get a recorded cassette from their son's secretary every year telling them precisely what time they can contact him. It's right considerate.

"For instance, if I ever meet him, he's always got two people there to greet me. His minder and his agent. People are always coming up to Jon Jon with pieces of paper, and you can never be too careful. You can never tell when it might be some

dodgy con artist trying to get Jon to put his name to Vince Hill's Larynx Lozenges or something. That's why he's always got his minder with him, it keeps out the riff raff.

"Like the time I was once round at his flat. Well, I was next door actually, 'cos Jon had an important meeting with a manicurist at the time. Anyway the building was absolutely besieged by John Benson fans hoping for a glimpse of their hero. They'd got the wrong address and were seething. So Jon has to be careful – who knows, Michael Aspel might disguise himself as me when he catches Jon Jon out for the *This Is Your Life* show they're bound to do. My Jonathan is so considerate.

"He came round to see me last year.

We didn't talk too much 'cos he was doing an interview for some kids magazine, *NME* or something. He kept talking about street cred and what it was like growing up in a tower block, which was a bit of a white lie. I only moved here when I couldn't keep up with the mortgage repayments. It was my own fault really, I didn't read the fine print.

"You see I was short of a few bob and I asked Jon for a loan. He didn't hesitate, not him. His hand jumped into his pocket and pulled out a tenner. All I had to do was sign a note promising to pay him back within a year. I didn't read the stuff in invisible ink about the rate of interest not being less than the rate of inflation in Mexico or something. I had to sell everything, but Jon, ever the faithful son, gave me a very good price.

"And you know with some of the money he made out of selling my furniture he did a great re-touching job on one of our family portraits. There's me and dad and Jon, only he got an artist friend of his to montage the face of Marilyn Monroe on me and Sean Connery on dad. Jon Jon shows the picture to all his friends. He says it looks better, and I agree with him. It's so thoughtful of him, he only wants it to look good."

# THE ONES THEY BANNED
## TV INTERVIEWS YOU NEVER SAW

### ● KIM PHILBY

**JR:** Let's face it, Kim, it must be really horrible living in Russia. No shops, no designer clothes, concentration camps. Don't you regret it really?

**KIM PHILBY:** (Deeply anxious. Eyes darting fearfully into the wings) You must let me tell you who was the fifth man! Please! Before it's too late!

**JR:** I mean, it's true, isn't it, that every Russian leader since the Revolution has worn the same suit, right?

**KIM PHILBY:** (Panicky) They're trying to kill me! I want to help my country. Don't let me take these secrets to the grave!

**JR:** And the shoes, right – isn't it true they're made of cardboard?

**KIM PHILBY** (Gushing) It's Geoffrey Howe!

**JR:** Tell us a bit more about the haircuts.

**KIM PHILBY:** (Gushing blood) Aaaaaaaaagggggghhhhhhhh!!!!!

**JR:** Well there you have it, ladies and gentlemen. Kim Philby… er… (Shuffles through notes)… from the Moscow State Circus.

**APPLAUSE**

### HOW THEY BANNED IT

Telephone rings.
The Chairman of the IBA picks up the receiver.

**GEOFFREY HOWE:** Hello, John. Bit of rescheduling, I'm afraid.

**CHAIRMAN:** Sure, fine, no problem.

**GEOFFREY:** The Jonathan Ross interview…

**CHAIRMAN:** Yes?

**GEOFFREY:** Lose it, will you, old boy.

**CHAIRMAN:** Christ! Of course! Jesus – thank God you rang! Blimey! I'm really sorry. Really really sorry!!
Telephone clicks.

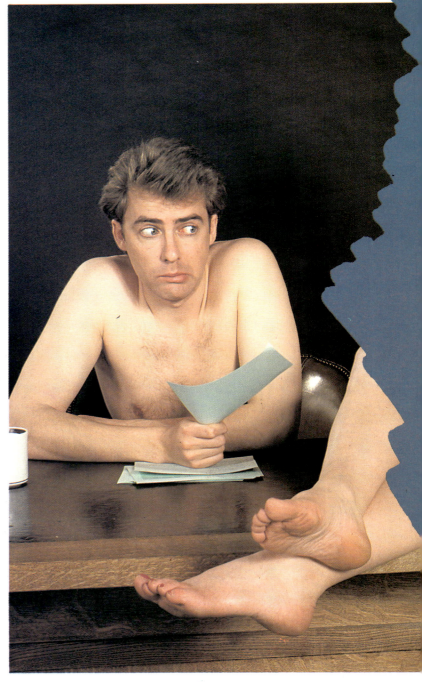

# ROSS ON ROSS

**JR:** So, Jonathan, do you enjoy working in television?

**JR:** Not particularly, Jonathan, do you?

**JR:** Television? I can't get enough of it!

**JR:** What do you mean? You're contradicting what I just said.

**JR:** So? I like my job. Do you want me to lie?

**JR:** But you're me – you have to agree with everything I say.

**JR:** Fascist!

**JR:** You should know.

**JR:** Look stupid – we won't get anywhere at all by bickering like this.

**JR:** Get on with it then ... fatso!

**JR:** OK, um... what's your favourite colour?

**JR:** Er... can't we start with something a bit easier?

## DR SCROTE WRITES:

*Looking back at interviews such as this it is easy now to see the signs of latent schizophrenia in the patient. In the light of the accusations of professional negligence levelled at me subsequent to Mr Ross's committal, I would like to point out that at the time of the interview it seemed nothing more than normal, high-spirited behaviour, and the fact that Jonathan went on to beat himself up I interpreted as a tribute to one of his favourite film directors, Michael Winner. Furthermore, Channel 4 only banned the programme on the grounds that Jonathan was not allowed to knife himself before the eleven o'clock watershed.*

**MAY 25th** Someone keeps ringing then hanging up as soon as I answer. My manager says it's the hounds of Fleet Street who are after my blood now that I'm a celebrity. I'm a bit worried that this diary might fall into the wrong hands, so from now on I'm going to be a lot more careful what I write.

**MAY 26th** Met Sabrina for lunch at the Savoy. Afterwards retired to her hotel room where we proceeded to have an extremely interesting conversation about Central American politics. Afterwards I was so exhausted I could barely stand, so I took a taxi to Frank's where he gave me a couple of games of squash to perk me up.

**MAY 27th** Had lunch with Jeffrey Archer today. What a nice man – and *such* a talented writer! However, I couldn't help noticing what a smooth skin he had and this rather put me off my goat's cheese ravioli.

**MAY 28th** Willingly went to my fave nitespot Stringfellows with my shy, but honest manager, Gary. As well as some of those terrifically erudite fellows who work for certain Sunday papers, who should I see but Joan Collins? What an amazing woman – I have only to think of her and it gives me a stiffy.

**MAY 29th** I'm bored with being so careful all the time – to hell with it. My fans love me, the newspapers love me, the people at Channel Four love me. I'm just going to be myself and forget all this crap about being discreet.

**MAY 30th** Went to a little massage parlour old Putters told me about. Later as I left with Ron and Nigel I could have sworn someone took my photo, but perhaps it was just the light playing tricks on my eyes.

**MAY 31st**

**Shit!**

**JUNE 12th** Feeling a bit perkier now all the trouble over the back rub's starting to die down. Received a letter from a Mr Terry Wogan offering me the benefit of his long experience as a broadcaster and TV personality. He gave me a number of very useful suggestions – unfortunately most of them are illegal, and anyway I've always been rather fond of guppies.

**JUNE 13th** I realised it's puppies I'm fond of, not guppies, and so I took TW's advice. Not bad, but a bit sticky, and it ruined my creases.

**JUNE 14th** Apparently a photographer from the *News of the World* was lurking by the pond yesterday. I fear a scandal is looming.

**JUNE 15th** One teensy-weensy mistake and the whole world turns on you. In the face of vociferous protest and immense pressure from the tabloid press there was only one honourable course of action open to me. I shopped Terry.

**JUNE 16th** Terry has issued a statement to the press. He says the only advice he ever offered me concerned young upwardly mobile professional women, not fish.

**JUNE 17th** My manager has told the papers I'm an ichthyologist – a fish expert – and that I often hang out by ponds in the hope of spotting some tiddlers. He made me go and pose with some haddocks in Billingsgate market. Some-times I wish I was dead.

# Toady

# NOTHING FISHY ABOUT ME!

Cheeky TV chatster Jonathan Ross was full of *fish 'n' quips* today as he posed with Harry the Hake, a recent guest on The Last Resort. Earlier this week Ross, 28, labelled rumours of bizarre sexual practices involving young fish *"Codswallop"*. Jonathan, a confirmed bachelor, told the press, "If you don't want me to sue you you'd better get your *skates* on and publish a retraction!" You name the time, Jonathan, we'll name the *plaice*!!!!

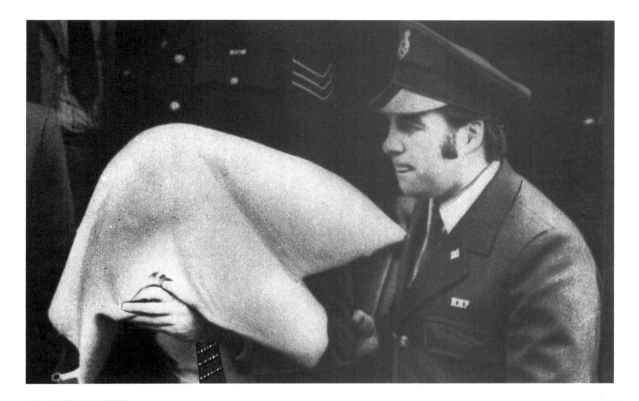

**NOVEMBER 15th** It just seems to be one damaging scandal after another at the moment. Now some flake calling himself Dr. Schröte has sold the Fleet Street vipers what he claims are secret papers belonging to and written by me. Somebody somewhere is out to get me.

**NOVEMBER 16th** I will always be grateful to the few kind people who have stood by me in this my hour of need. As for the others! Huh! Call themselves true showbiz friends! This morning Dickie Henderson snubbed me in the street, and this afternoon at the golf club my dear old chum Tarby pointedly refused to let me borrow his mashie niblick.

**NOVEMBER 17th** My birthday! Held a party in the Palm Room at the Waldorf Astoria. Nobody came.

**NOVEMBER 18th** Sat in bed all day, crying. My solicitors have sent me a copy of the press statement we are issuing to counter the latest vicious round of rumour and innuendo. I hope people find it convincing, otherwise I'm really finished.

# Hess, Mengele & Ribbentrop

## Solicitors

PRESS STATEMENT

THE VON ROSS DIARIES:
Why They're Fakes.

Here once and for all we would like to take the
opportunity to refute the allegations that have
been levelled at our client, Mr Ross, and to dispel
the mass of damaging and, we submit, libellous
press claims about the so called 'Von Ross Diaries'
and Mr Ross's implied involvement with the Third
Reich.

We herein offer irrefutable evidence that this
document is nothing but a heinous forgery.

THE FACTS

1. The Ross family has never had a 'von' in their
   name. Dr. Schröte has probably either become
   confused by Jonathan's cousin Yvonne Ross, or
   has fallen into the trap — so easy for a
   foreigner — of misunderstanding the words of
   Jonathan himself. "Hello and welcome to the Last
   Resort. My name is Jonavon Ross"...
2. Jonathan cannot write in German. In actual fact,
   Jonathan cannot even write in English.
3. Jonathan has never owned a black shirt. And if
   he had done it is inconceivable that he would
   have worn it with the type of armbands the
   Doctor describes.
4. Hitler was born in 1889. Jonathan Ross was born
   in 1960. A significant difference.
5. When Jonathan publicly declared on TV that, "I
   won't make the same mistakes next time I invade
   Poland," he was only joking.

On behalf of Jonathan Ross we challenge anyone to
find a shred of definite proof to link him with
these incriminating diaries.

R. Hess of Hess, Mengele and Ribbentrop (Solicitors)

## JONATHAN'S LAST RESORT?

Jonathan Ross's recently sacked manager today refused to deny rumours that his former client was staying at an exclusive celebrity rehabilitation clinic somewhere in the Home Counties. When asked to comment about the recent split with Ross he replied, "Who cares about that untalented shite? With John Benson as my client things have never looked brighter."

Ross associates report that in the days and weeks following the latest press scandal and the subsequent cancellation of his TV series, Jonathan Ross has become a shadow of his former self. Reclusive, overweight and prone to bouts of excessive curry-eating, his few friends think that seeking professional help is Ross's last resort.

"Champers Health Spa"

**DECEMBER 1st**  This is it! My week at Champers Health Spa begins. I intend to return either as my old self or as a new man – whichever turns out sexier.

**DECEMBER 2nd**  Very little time to write a thing in here. They keep you busy all the time and you aren't allowed to go out. No alcohol, plenty of exercise and healthy food. Went to bed feeling sick.

**DECEMBER 3rd**  Feel worse today. Got cramp during the morning swim and was rewarded with a small tub of plain yoghurt. Ugh! What's more, they have confiscated my swimming trunks for being "unhygienic". Ha! They're just about fifty times sexier than everyone else's, that's all. Some of the fatties in this place make Bernard Manning look like Lena Zavaroni.

**DECEMBER 4th**  Ran into the entire Channel Four racing unit in the high security vegan-wing dining room. They certainly need treatment like a duck needs webbed feet.

**DECEMBER 5th**  Last night I dreamt about the girl in the Flake ad. We were lying in a field of scarlet poppies when a dark cloud covered the sun and large drops of rain began to fall on us. Suddenly the bitch grabbed my Flake and scoffed the lot without even offering me a bite. Woke up at 4.00am to the sound of screams. I was worried they might be my own, but this morning someone told me the terrible commotion was only Angela Rippon being taken away to a "safer" sanatorium.

**DECEMBER 6th**  The ITN boys left today in a chorus of sad farewells – though some of them did shout, "See you after Christmash darling," to the head of the nursing staff as their ambulance pulled down the drive.

I must say all this healthy living is beginning to make me feel what must be my old self. Not too sure that's why I didn't leave it in the first place.

**DECEMBER 7th**  I leave Champers cured, slim and rested, and feeling positive and optimistic about the future. Stop in a little pub in Bray on the way back to London...

Why I refuse
to have
my picture
in this
book

By
**BERNARD
MANNING**

I refuse to have my picture in *Go To Bed With Jonathan Ross* for the following reasons:  Nobody asked me  Nobody offered me money 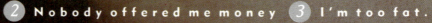 3 I'm too fat.

# CHAPTER EIGHT

## 1989-?

### In the Future Anything Is Possible

**WRITTEN BY** Lise Mayer, Jim Reid and Jonathan Ross

**DESIGNED BY** Zoltan Marfy at The Shape Of Things

**PHOTOGRAPHS BY** Howard Tyler

**ILLUSTRATIONS BY** Dave Eastbury and Mike Nicholson

**EDITED BY** Cat Ledger

**ADDITIONAL MATERIAL BY** Simon Bell, Jon Canter, Simon Greenall, Chris Lang, Alan Marke, Rowland Rivron and Graham K. Smith

**PHOTO LOVE BY** Viz

**LAST RESORT PHOTOS:** Sven Arnstein

**SPECIAL THANKS TO** David and Sally Beer, John Benson, Mike Bolland, Seamus Cassidy, Harry Enfield, Ewart Studios, Gary Farrow, Clive Frampton, Jane Goldman, Tony Harpur, Lauren Laurent, Nathalie Laurent Marke, Debbie Marrow, Steve Nieve and the Playboys, Rose Nielsen, Rick and Heidi Paxton, Alev Reid, Dexter Sayle, Alison Taylor, Paul Whitehouse, Iris Wilkes and Very Special Thanks to Mum and Dad and all the Little Rosses

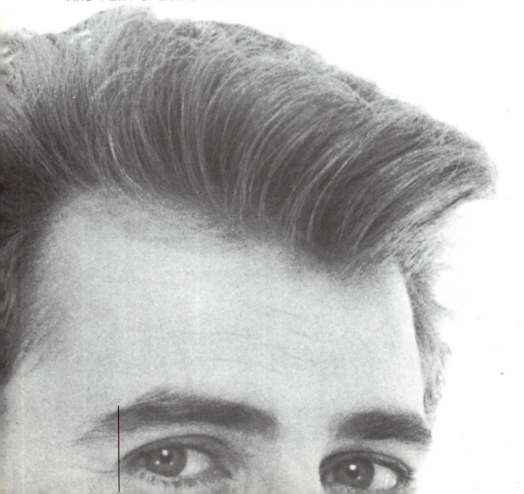